# Tracks of the White-Tailed Buck

## A Deer Tracking & Hunting Guide

Development and Use of:

### THE TRACKOMETER

*The Original White-Tail Buck Track Scale*

**By Wayne A. Laroche**

Published By

Stonefish Environmental

2439 Lake Road

Franklin, Vermont 05457

www.trackometer.com

Email: whitetails@trackometer.com

*Library of Congress Control Number: 2011941690*

ISBN: 978-0-9839830-0-2

*Printed in the United States of America*

# Contents

# Preface: The TRACKOMETER

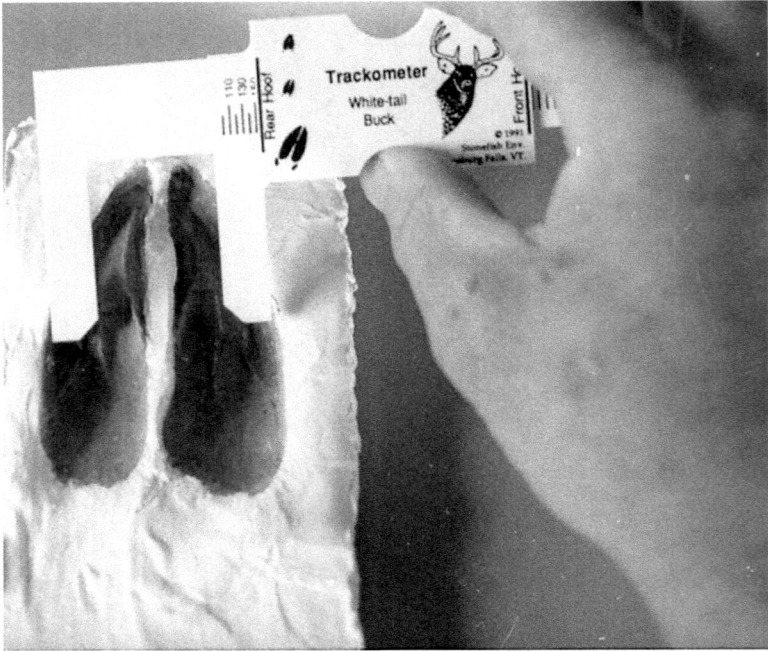

**Figure 1  Measure Track to Estimate Dressed Weight of Buck**

The TRACKOMETER is a tool for estimating the weight of whitetail bucks by measuring their tracks. The TRACKOMETER'S unique scales accurately estimate a buck's weight by measuring the width of his tracks or hoofs.

The TRACKOMETER's scales read in pounds "dressed weight" which is the weight of the carcass having the heart, liver, lung, and all viscera removed. Terms used by hunters to describe carcass weight vary from region to region across North America. "Field dressed" in some regions is termed "hog dressed" in other regions."

The idea leading to development of the TRACKOMETER came from reading magazine articles that claimed no one could tell how big a buck was by its tracks.  Having hunted and tracked deer most of my life, I was skeptical of these claims. Being a biologist having dealt with length/weight and other body proportion relationships among a variety of fish and wildlife species, I knew that the body weight of animals often correlates with dimensions of body parts. So, I expected that there was a good chance that some dimension of a deer's hoof could vary with the weight of a deer. I set about measuring deer hoofs at deer check stations, lockers and any other place that I could find a buck to measure. I collected measurements from more than 100 whitetail bucks ranging from 90 to 244 lbs. dressed weight. The scales of the TRACKOMETER were created based on these measurements.

Although millions of hunters have used tracks and other sign to scout for and hunt whitetail deer through the ages, amazingly little has been written about the structure of deer feet and characteristics of the tracks they make. Tracks and other sign left by whitetails, not only provide trails that a hunter can track and follow, they also provide evidence that describes and records deer behavior.

Feeding, resting, tending fawns, seeking does, chasing does, breeding and every other behavior that a deer engages in during the course of its' life are "written" across the landscape in the form of tracks, feces, urine, beds, scrapes, rubs, clipped and broken vegetation, blood, hair, and scent. Characterized as either disturbances of the landscape or as materials left behind, deer sign provides clues and evidence of deer activity. Like a crime scene investigator, a good tracker learns to "read" the history of events that lead to the end of a trail, and perhaps, the buck of a life-time.

Whether you just want to learn more about deer sign to help with your pre-season scouting or you are interested in learning more about tracking big bucks in the big woods, this book and the TRACKOMETER provide the tools you need.

The TRACKOMETER can be purchased via the web at www. TRACKOMETER.COM. This web site also provides additional photos as well as videos on tracking white-tailed deer.

A good tracker has many skills.

# Introduction

Every creature that moves across the face of the earth leaves behind tracks or other signs of its passing. The white-tailed deer is no exception. Deer leave an abundance of sign as they go about their lives. Sign is left as either disturbances in the environment that an animal passes through or materials that an animal leaves behind such as its droppings, urine or pieces of hair. Signs of passage range from things that are highly visible like buck rubs, scrapes and droppings to things that are completely invisible to the naked eye such as the trail of skin cells and scent molecules that a beagle follows in pursuit of a snowshoe hare. These signs are more or less ephemeral in time; they don't last long. Sign decays, ages or gets covered over and buried with the passage of time.

Under exceptional conditions fossil tracks have been found to exist for millions of years. Tracks in deer country usually disappear much more quickly. The forces of nature destroy them as time passes.

Physical, chemical and biological forces of nature begin decaying, eroding, evaporating, scattering and covering animal sign moments after it is left behind. Rain, snow, sunshine, wind and other animals constantly work to reshape the surface of the earth. The rate at which sign decays or is covered varies and depends on the relative timing, duration and magnitude of these forces. For this reason, tracks and other sign age at different rates.

Aging tracks and other sign is not always simple. But, the state of decay that sign exists in at any point in time does provide valuable clues to how long the decaying process has been going on. If you know how long the decaying process has been underway, you have a way of determining when the animal made tracks or left sign behind. To age tracks and sign, it is necessary to couple observations of state of decay with knowledge of relative and actual timing of events that cause sign to decay at different rates.

If you know what to look for, the tracks and sign left in passing by an animal can tell you a lot about the animal and its behavior. You can tell the size and sex of a deer by the shape and pattern of tracks. You can tell what the animal was doing by observing a trail of tracks. You can tell the sex of the animal by urine stains, buck rubs, and many other indicators. You can even tell the size of an animal. In fact, the

TRACKOMETER for whitetail bucks can be used to measure tracks and estimate the weight of bucks.

Sounds pretty technical? It can be. But, don't worry. Some of best deer trackers that I have known are unable to explain the technical details. They see, sense, feel and react to signs within the environment perhaps even on some subconscious level. Their natural powers of observation work for them. They track and take big bucks every year. The problem is: they can't always teach others how to do it like they do.

It doesn't matter whether you live in the north where snow tracking is possible or south where snow is a novelty, if you hunt whitetails, you should be paying attention to deer tracks and sign. It doesn't matter whether your preferred hunting style is stand hunting, tracking, stalking or calling. As you learn about white-tailed deer and develop your hunting skills, your love, enjoyment and appreciation for hunting and wildlife will grow as well.

I have spent more than forty years tracking and hunting whitetail deer. Much of the fun was in the learning. In this guide, I am going to provide details that will help you learn to better recognize and use deer tracks and other sign to scout and hunt white-tailed deer. I will also explain how the TRACKOMETER deer track measuring tool can further help by providing an objective way to judge the size of a buck and his tracks.

## Development of the TRACKOMETER

I learned a lot about deer when I set out to develop the TRACKOMETER. To share what I have learned, I am going to begin by explaining how the TRACKOMETER was developed as well as the details about hoofs and tracks that I learned during the process.

I set out to develop the scales for TRACKOMETER by measuring and observing hoofs and tracks of white-tail bucks harvested in northeastern North America. All bucks were taken within the range of the whitetail subspecies *Odocoileus virginianus borealis* which is one of sixteen North American subspecies. It should be noted that in parts of the country where other whitetail subspecies exist that the scales of TRACKOMETER could be miscalibrated. You should keep this in mind if you hunt in other parts of North America where different subspecies of whitetails exist. Regardless of possible subspecies differences, the TRACKOMETER should still be useful as a scouting tool for whitetails everywhere because it can be used to judge the relative size of whitetail bucks even if weights happen to vary among whitetail subspecies.

Initially, several different hoof measurements were assessed to find which had the best correlation to body weight. Maximum hoof width was found to have the best relationship to body weight (for the geeks reading this, linear regression R-square values were just greater than 0.7). The TRACKOMETER provides estimates of weight from measurements of tracks with typical accuracy of about $\pm10\%$ of dressed body weight. Estimation error seems to be most commonly caused by weight loss due to rutting activity or weight loss due to dehydration between the time of kill and time of weighing a deer

**Measurements were made on bucks of known weight.**

**Bucks were weighted on certified scales at deer check stations.**

Measurements were taken on bucks harvested from early archery seasons through late firearms seasons that spanned the rut. Measurements from bucks during pre-rut, rut, and post-rut periods were pooled together. For this reason, the scales best estimate average expected weights of bucks during the fall breeding season. The ±10% error in estimation of body weight agrees well with published scientific research which has reported that mature bucks often lose 20% to 30% of their body weight during the rut.

Expect more over-estimates of weight using the TRACKOMETER during the pre-rut. Expect more under-estimates of weight during the post-rut.

Other factors must explain estimation error to some lesser degree. These factors may include error in measurement of track width, genetic variation, local differences in availability and quality of feed and nutrients, old age, disease or injuries that affect body weight.

4

# Anatomy of Hoofs and Tracks

Early in the process of measuring deer hoofs, I found that the front hoofs are almost always wider than rear hoofs on bucks weighing more than 150 lbs dressed weight. The difference in size between front and rear hoofs continues to increase as bucks get heavier.

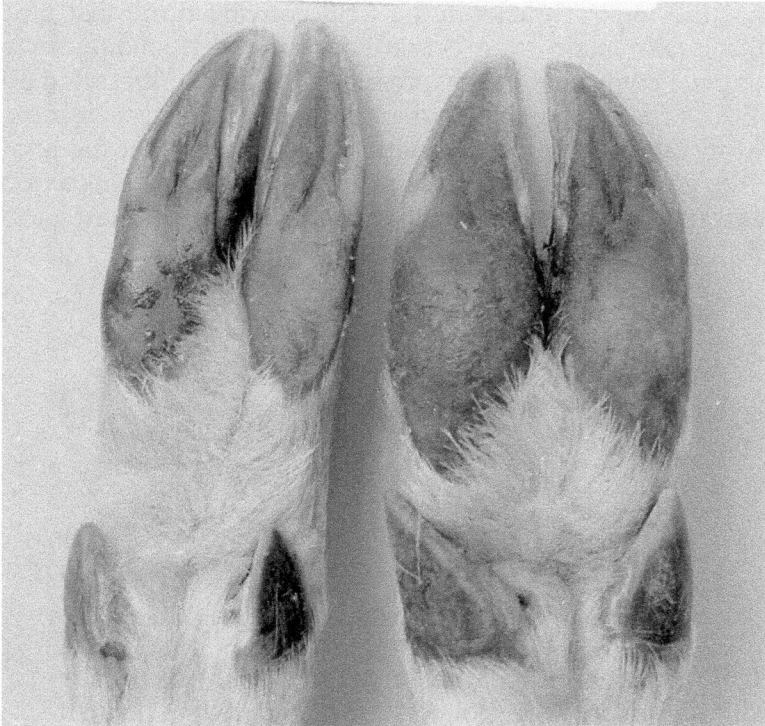

**Rear hoof (left) is typically narrower than front hoof (right).  Dew claws on the front feet are closer to the hoof than the dew claws of rear feet.  These are the feet of a buck that weighted 180 pounds.**

This was news to me at the time. But, when I examined the scientific literature, I found that other biologists had noted this characteristic of deer.  From my experience talking to hunters and reading hunting articles, it seems clear that the fact that front hoofs of big bucks are larger than rear hoofs has never been well known among hunters. Because a hunter may find different size tracks made by the different hoofs of a single buck, it is understandable that this could be confusing. Without doubt, differences in hoof size have added to the confusion among hunters and hindered recognition of the relationship between deer track size and deer weight among hunters.

I recall having followed tracks of many walking deer that suddenly appeared bigger after the deer started running. The size of the tracks didn't change. Clear tracks of he larger front hoofs simply became visible.

A close look at tracks in the field convinced me that the length of the tracks made by a deer's hoof varies depending on ground hardness. I confirmed this by pressing deer hoofs into soil to different depths. Variation in track length is caused by the curved shape of the back of a deer's hoof and variation in the depth that the hoof sinks into the ground surface. Tracks made by deer hoofs appear longer in soft ground or snow than on harder surfaces such as hard packed dirt roads.

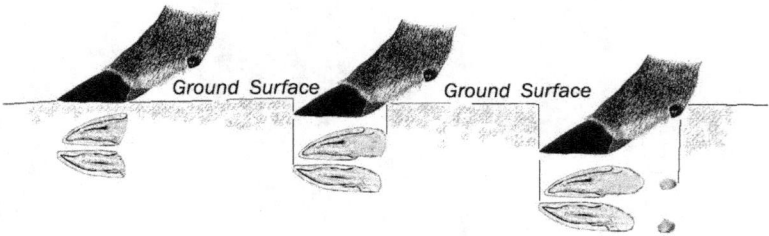

**Track length increases as hoofs sink deeper.**

This variation in track length caused by differences in the depth that hoofs sink into the ground surface will always make track length a subjective and unreliable measure of a deer's size.

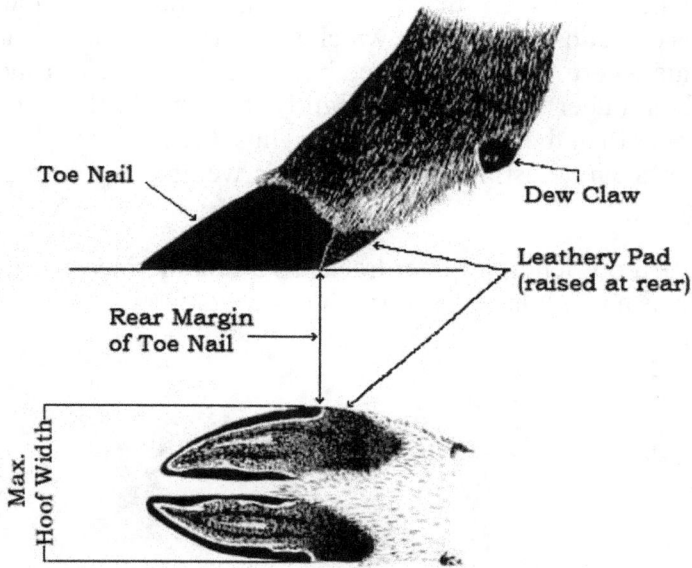

**Characteristics of deer feet.**

If you have read many hunting magazines or listened to deer camp tales through the course of your life, you may have heard that swamp dwelling bucks have sharp pointed hoofs as opposed to mountain bucks that have blunt, rounded hoofs. The folk lore suggests that deer walking on rocky mountain slopes tend to wear and chip off the tips of their toes more than deer living in swamplands where ground conditions are soft and rock free. Thus, their toes become rounded as they wear.

I haven't collected any hard data to either verify or falsify these reports. However, I can confirm that the toes of bucks are commonly worn and chipped, particularly on front hoofs of large bucks. Wear at the tips of the toes must tend to shorten hoofs and make track length an even more unreliable measure of a buck's weight. Besides wear caused by rocky soil, crusted snow also causes chipping and wears the tips of the hoofs. The scrape making process mostly involves use of the front hoofs. This may explain why the front hoofs of bigger bucks seem to have more wear and rounding of the toe tips on front hoofs compared to rear hoofs.

Even when tracks are made in snow and entirely visible, it is sometimes difficult to determine which toe is actually longest and the exact points where the tip of the toe begins and the back of the hoof ends. When a deer slips forward slightly in its track, the track may appear longer than the hoof really was. Thus, the ability to develop a method for accurate estimation of a buck's weight from hoof length is unlikely.

So, I ruled out length of deer tracks as a reliable measure of hoof length and as a potential estimator of deer weight.

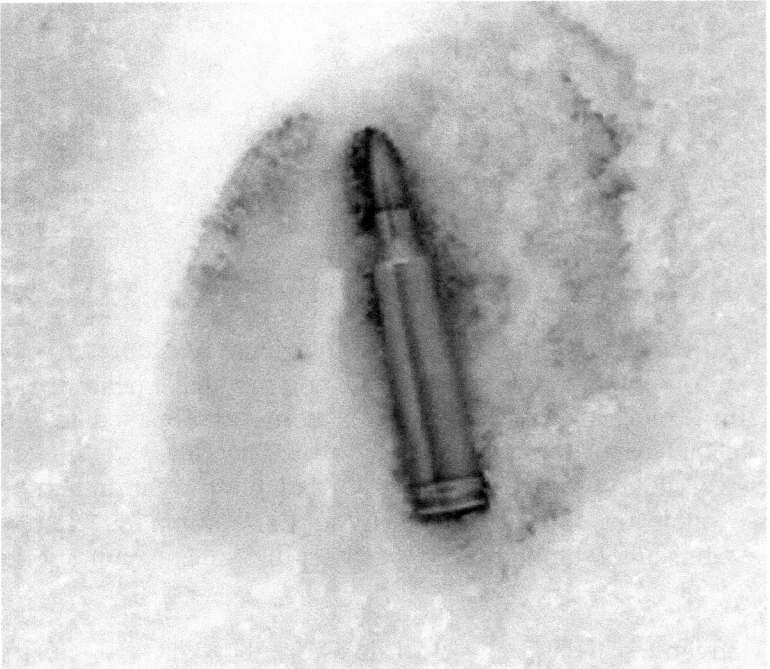

**The old rifle cartridge in the deer track method is an unreliable measure of the size of a track. It does not work.**

Unlike track length, track width doesn't share these problems. Track width doesn't vary with changes in ground condition and sinking depth. Maximum track width can be accurately measured even under hard ground conditions that result in only a partial print of the front half of the hoof because maximum track width occurs near the middle of the hoof at the back of the flat part of the hoof. The sides of deer hooves are not subject to differential wear as are the tips of the toes. Sides of the deer hoofs leave clear impressions that are easily and accurately measured and that are not as subject to slippage which generally occurs in the forward direction.

For these reasons, I concluded that hoof and track width maximum track width are the most useful measurements for estimating deer weight from hoofs and tracks. This discovery was the basis for development of the TRACKOMETER.

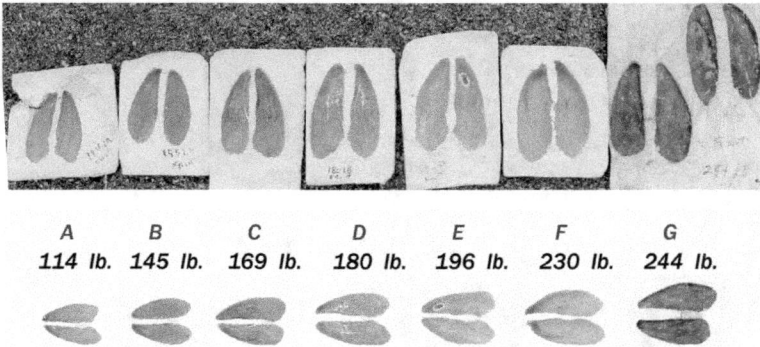

| A | B | C | D | E | F | G |
|---|---|---|---|---|---|---|
| 114 lb. | 145 lb. | 169 lb. | 180 lb. | 196 lb. | 230 lb. | 244 lb. |

**Plaster of Paris molds made from buck hoofs and arranged by weight of the buck. The top photo was cut and re-arranged to demonstrate that hoof width definitely increases with body weight.**

**Below are photographs of each buck from which these molds were made.**

**G-244 lb**           **F-230 lb**

**E-196 lb**

**D-180 lb**

**C-169 lb**

**B-145 lb**

**A-114 lb**

# How to Use of the TRACKOMETER

The TRACKOMETER is a tool used to estimate the dressed weight of whitetail bucks by measuring the maximum width of tracks or feet. To use the TRACKOMETER follow these steps:

1. Determine whether a track is from front or rear hoof. [All clearly visible walking tracks are tracks of the rear hoof that cover the front hoof print. Dew claws of front feet nearly touch the back of the hoof, especially in large bucks. The rearward prints of running deer tracks are the prints of the front hoofs.]

2. Make sure the track has toes spread by about the width of a pencil or ¼ inch. If the spread is too wide or narrow, find another track.

3. Place the jaws of the TRACKOMETER into track and spread the jaws until they span the maximum width of the track.

4. Read estimated weight from the TRACKOMETER scale. For greatest estimation accuracy, measure tracks from different hoofs and average the values.

The TRACKOMETER has both scales printed on the caliper arm.

Front hoofs of whitetail bucks are wider than rear hoofs, for this reason the TRACKOMETER was developed with two different scales for front and rear hoof tracks. Measuring either a front or rear hoof track using the appropriate scale will provide the best estimate of body weight. For greatest accuracy, first determine whether a track was made by a front or a rear hoof and measure more than one track.

In deep snow, it may be necessary to carefully clear snow away in order to insert the TRACKOMETER into the track. Put your hand into the track and push snow up and outward. Fluffy snow may require that you use your fingers to find where the track has been made in the ground surface below the snow. You can also try to find better tracks for measuring under trees where snow depth tends to be shallower.

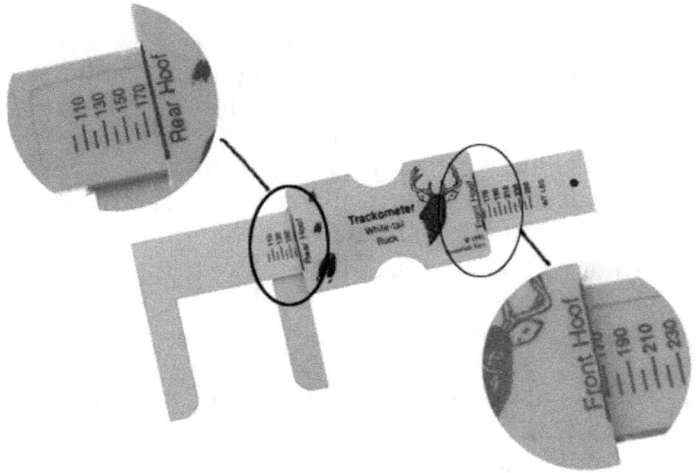

**Read Front or Rear Scale to measure front or rear hoof tracks.**

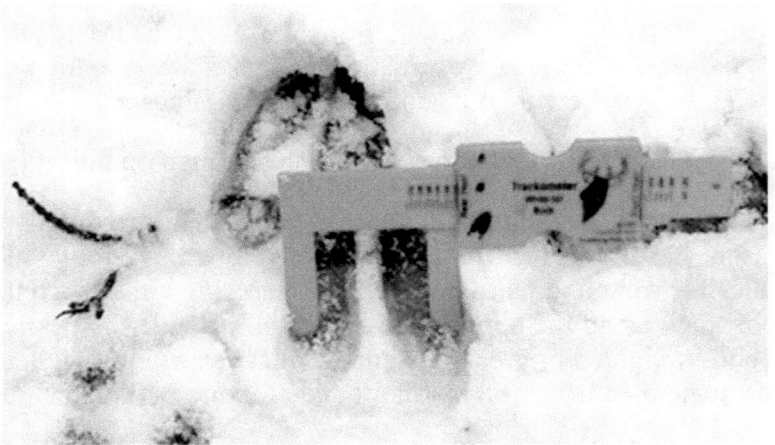

**Measuring rear track from buck weighting about 210 lbs. dressed weight which would be about 320 lbs. live weight.**

Sometimes hunters weight their deer before the heart and liver are removed from the carcass. As a rule of thumb, subtract 5 lbs. for deer weighing less than 150 lbs., 7 lbs. for deer weighing 150-200 lbs., and 9 lbs. for deer weighting 200-250 lbs. to adjust for this.

The following table provides approximate dressed weight to live weight conversions.

| Dressed Weight | Live Weight | Dressed Weight | Live Weight |
|---|---|---|---|
| 90 | 122 | 250 | 325 |
| 100 | 135 | 260 | 337 |
| 110 | 148 | 270 | 350 |
| 120 | 160 | 280 | 363 |
| 130 | 173 | 290 | 375 |
| 140 | 186 | 300 | 388 |
| 150 | 198 | 310 | 401 |
| 160 | 211 | 320 | 413 |
| 170 | 224 | 330 | 426 |
| 180 | 236 | 340 | 439 |
| 190 | 249 | 350 | 451 |
| 200 | 262 | 360 | 464 |
| 210 | 274 | 370 | 477 |
| 220 | 287 | 380 | 489 |
| 230 | 300 | 390 | 502 |
| 240 | 312 | 400 | 515 |

# Tracks, Trails and Hoofs

Walking deer place their rear hoofs into the tracks of the front hoofs. When you look at a trail of walking deer tracks, all distinct imprints are tracks of the rear hoofs that have stepped on and overlay the tracks of the front hoofs. While the rear hoof tracks of some deer almost perfectly overlay the front tracks, the stride of some deer does not result in a perfect overlay. When this happens, a partial print of the front hoof is visible.

**Distinct tracks of walking deer are all tracks of hind feet. Tracks of front feet are covered by the tracks of hind feet.**

Tracks made by front hoofs can usually be seen clearly when made by running deer; made by a buck making a scrape; or made by a deer that has made a rub or fed on trees or shrubs and then turned as it walked away.

**Tracks of front hoofs can be found where deer have approached vegetation to feed.**

When whitetails run, they swing the hind feet ahead of their front feet. The problem with measuring tracks from running deer is that the tips of the toes are often spread far apart. Remember, accurate measurements with the TRACKOMETER require tracks having the toes spread by about ¼ inch at the tips. The width of a pencil is a good measure for comparison. Usually, it is not necessary to follow a running deer far before it slows down enough to find a good walking track for measuring.

Measure several tracks from different hoofs of a deer and average the values to get the best estimate of weight. It is not unusual for a deer to have one hoof that is larger or smaller than the others

Tracks having widely spread toes are not suitable for measurement with the Trackometer. Look for a track with toes spread by about 1/4 inch. Note imprints of the dew claws.

Hind feet swing ahead of front feet when deer run.

**Top two tracks are imprints of the rear hoofs that have swung ahead of the front hoofs (bottom two tracks) of a running buck.**

Dew claws on the front feet are larger and closer to the hoof than dew claws on rear feet. As a deer's foot grows, the space, between the dew claws on the front foot and the rear margin of the hoof, narrows. Very large bucks have dew claws on the front foot extending all the way to the back of the hoof.

Tracks having dew claw imprints nearly touching the back of the hoof print are tracks of a front foot. Tracks having dew claw imprints two or three inches behind the hoof print are tracks made by hind feet. Imprints of dew claws are most obvious from running tracks because tracks are generally pressed deeper into the ground surface.

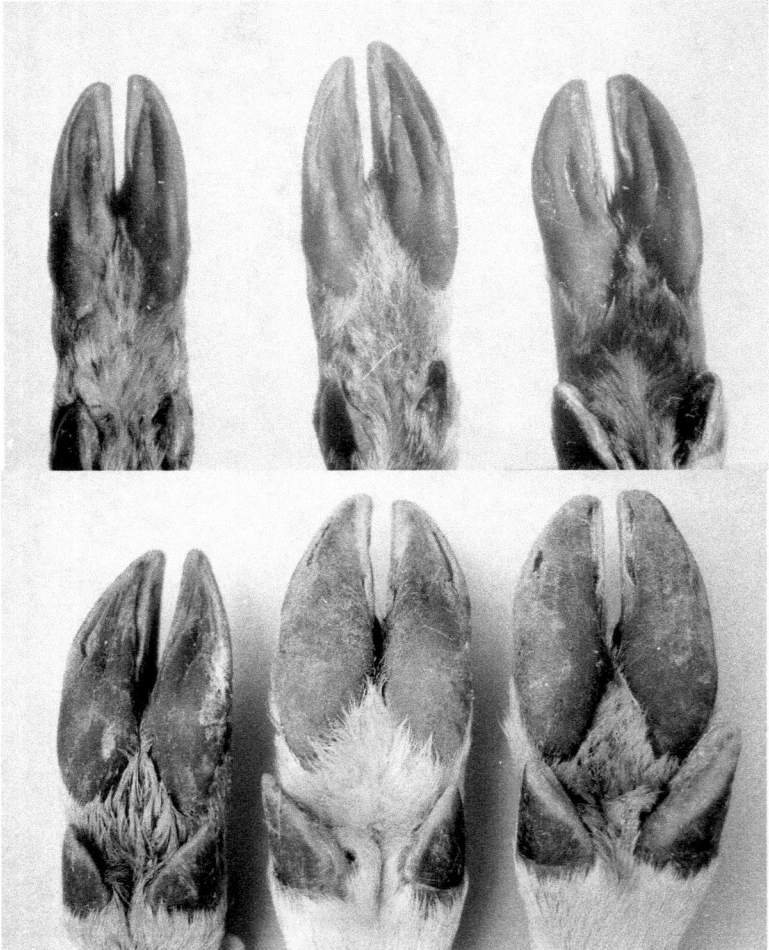

**Rear (Top) Front (Bottom)  Dew claws reach closer to the back of the hoof in bigger bucks.  Dew claws may overlap the back of the hoof on front hoofs of the biggest bucks.**

Tracks of big deer made on soft ground or snow have well defined imprints of the dew claws because hoofs sink deeply into the ground surface. Although I have heard deer camp arguments over whether or not tracks of dew claws mean that the tracks were made by a buck. Both bucks and does have dew claws. It is unlikely that imprints of dew claws can be used to help tell buck tracks from doe tracks or aid in the estimation of deer weight.

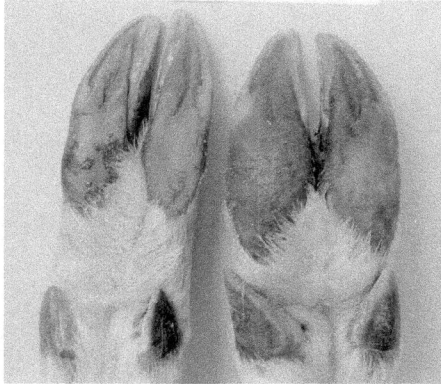

**Dew claws on rear hoof (left) are smaller and farther from the back of the hoof than dew claws on the front hoof (right).**

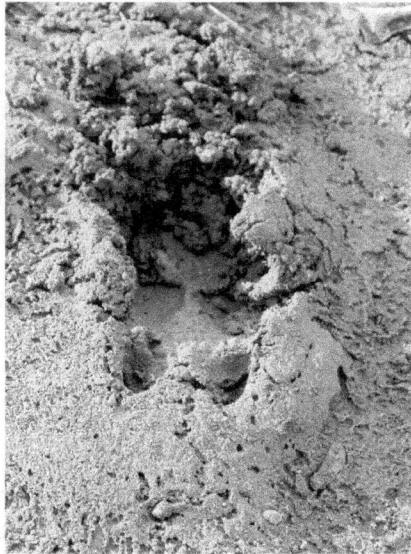

**Dew claw prints are made when hoofs sink deep in surface.**

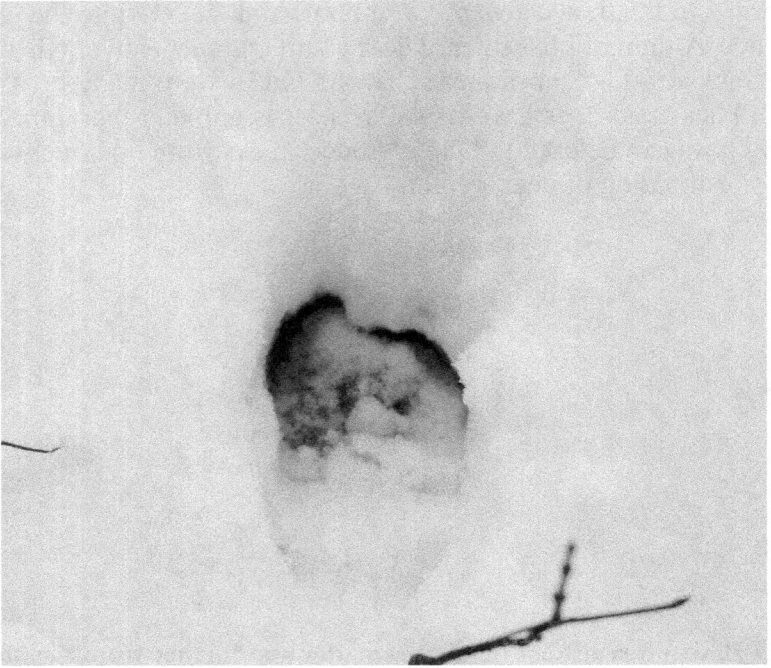

**A long toe on a hoof can leave a distinctive track that clearly identifies an individual buck.**

Although many magazine articles and hunting books have discussed the fact that large deer tracks cut deeper into the ground than tracks of small deer, all such accounts are anecdotal, subjective and of little practical use. It seems very unlikely that, even if precise and detailed measurements were taken, sinking depth could be used to estimate a deer's weight. Ground conditions, especially ground hardness, are simply too variable to provide for any consistent comparison to deer weight.

The TRACKOMETER is a handy tool for precisely measuring deer tracks. Coupling track measurements with other track characteristics such as relative length of toes and groove and ridge patterns makes it possible to identify individual bucks by their tracks. Measurement of track width and observation of other print characteristics is very useful for scouting and locating big bucks.

Whitetail bucks typically have home ranges of one to two square miles. Most of the year, mature bucks band together into buck groups of various sizes depending upon the density of bucks in an area. At deer densities between 10 and 30 deer per square mile, bucks groups typically range in size from two to seven bucks age 2+. So within any square mile of natural deer habitat at any time, there is a limited number of bucks. The likelihood of finding any two bucks within an area having all four hoofs measuring exactly the same width would seem fairly small even when twin brothers occur.

Actually, a deer's tracks are almost certainly as distinctive as the "finger prints" of humans. The bottom of deer hoofs have grooves and ridges that can be seen in tracks if the ground surface takes imprints well. These grooves and ridges are sharp and well-defined in young deer. As deer grow older and heavier, hoofs may become chipped and rounded at the tips causing the raised leathery pad at the rear of the hoof to bear more of the body's weight. Sometimes one toe is longer than the other on a foot. The four hoofs of a buck commonly differ somewhat in width. Front and rear hoofs of big bucks almost always differ in width. It is normal for even a pair of rear hoofs to have some difference in width. The same is true of front hoofs.

These oddities are imprinted in tracks when ground conditions are ideal. These characteristics along with readings from the TRACKOMETER provide the evidence needed to identify individual bucks by their tracks. You may find that the big buck that you are scouting has one rear hoof that is wider than the other. By using the TRACKOMETER, you may find a simple way to recognize and distinguish his track from the tracks of other bucks in your area.

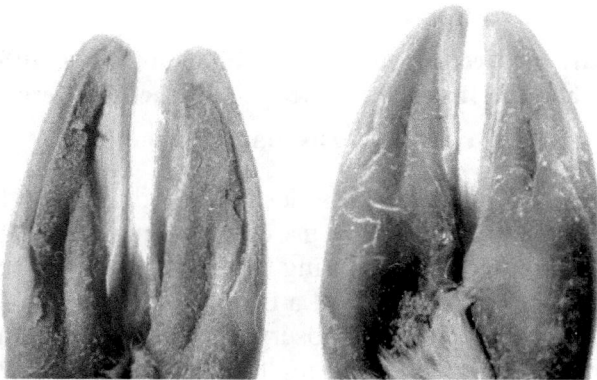

**Grooves, ridges, toe tip lengths and shapes are unique to each buck like the fingers and finger prints of humans. Note the differences.**

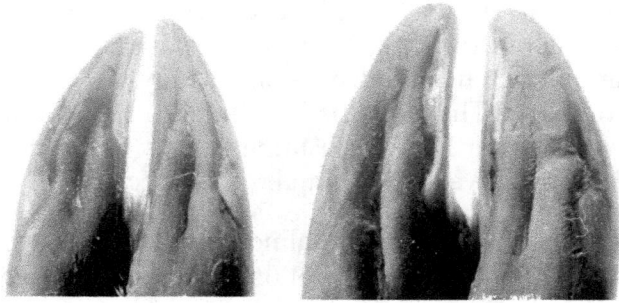

**Hoof oddities are imprinted in deer tracks and can be observed under the best tracking conditions.**

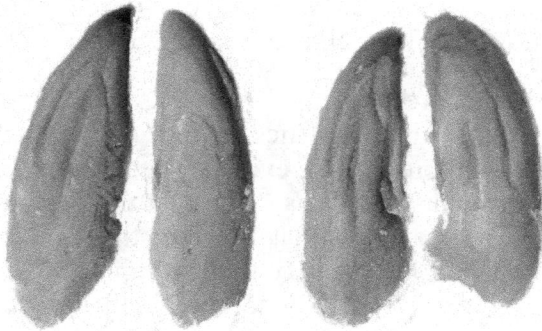

**Above are molded imprints of rear hoofs from two different bucks that weighed 160 lbs each. Notice the distinctly different groove and ridge patterns that each hoof has**

Scouting for big bucks provides another dimension to the hunting experience. Combined with the use of trail cameras, electronic mapping programs and GPS units, scouting for tracks will most certainly give a hunter an edge in the pursuit of a trophy whitetail buck. By carefully studying deer tracks, a good observer will be able to gather valuable information while scouting during the pre- and post-season as well as while tracking and hunting.

**Chipped hoofs provide distinctive track characteristics that can be
used to identify individual bucks.**

# Scouting for Tracks

One great thing about scouting for deer tracks and sign is that you can do it at any time of year. It is also good exercise, fun and will add a lot to your outdoor and hunting experience. If you enjoy outdoor photography or set game cameras to capture photos of bucks in your favorite hunting area, you either are or should be using tracks and other deer sign to guide your efforts. Tracks provide information about where deer have been and when they were there. By learning to "read" the sign deer leave behind, you may be able to get a good idea of when a deer might show up again.

During hot, dry weather in late summer and early fall, tracks are sometimes difficult to find because of dry, hard ground conditions. Look for tracks in wet areas along the edges of roads and fields and in feeding areas. Look in ditches, along stream banks, around beaver ponds, and anywhere in the woods where mud or soft ground can be found. Look for deer hair on barbed wire fences as this will often provide tell-tale clues to locations of deer crossings. Look for deer droppings. The state of decay of the pellets will provide clues whether deer are still using an area.

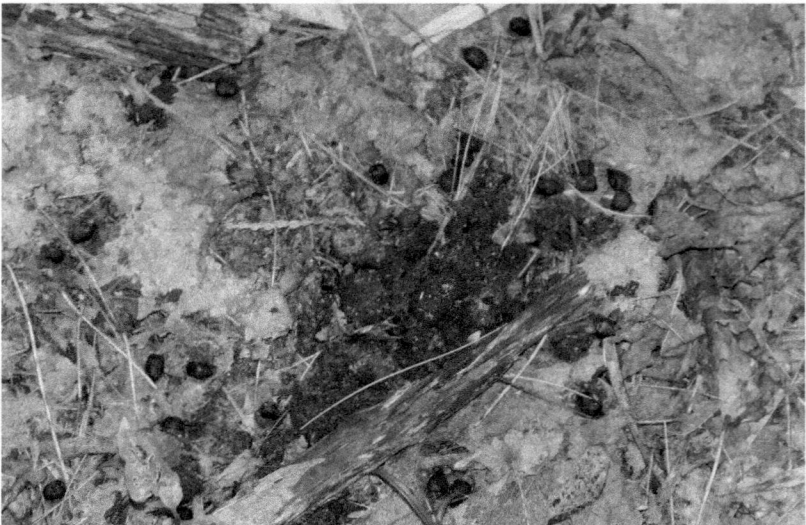

**Notice fresh deer pellets have been deposited over pellets in an advanced state of decay indicating that deer frequently use this area.**

Look for deer paths, tracks and other evidence of travel through grass and vegetation. By following faint trails through vegetation, you will often come to softer ground where tracks will be easier to see. Note the direction in which vegetation has been broken or bent to find clues to the direction of travel. Once you have located an area being used by deer, you can improve your ability to find tracks by clearing away old tracks along common travel routes and then returning later to note the time of day when new tracks appear.

Tracks provide a way of finding where a buck is traveling. They will help you find new places to put your trail cameras and your hunting stands.

If ground conditions are too hard to form good prints, you may be able to solve this problem by using a rake or short handled garden cultivator to scrape and loosen the soil. You may even want to wet the soil. Deer seem to be attracted to disturbed patches of earth as they are also attracted to scrapes. Actually, you may improve your ability to see tracks and take good pictures of deer by creating mock scrapes in front of your trail camera. Adding a little urine to the disturbed soil won't hurt. With a little luck, you will get a good shot of that big buck that you are looking for as well as a good look at his tracks. Take time to use the TRACKOMETER and take some track measurements. Also, look closely for any unique track characteristics, such as differing toe length or sharp versus rounded toes, that will allow you to recognize tracks of a specific buck if you come across them in other places that you scout.

"Patterning" is the word now used for the study of the travel patterns of deer. Deer do not move randomly about their home range. They concentrate their movements during certain times of the day and seasons of the year to satisfy daily and annual life requirements.

Use a small hand cultivator to create a good surface (mock scrape) where you can observe tracks of the bucks in your area. Pictures can make this even more interesting

**Trail of tracks across field left by buck heading for alfalfa field.**

Deer tend to react predictably to landform and vegetation patterns. They use the contours of the land and vegetation to shelter their movements and minimize effort spent while traveling. Deer travel along edges formed by changes in forest and other land cover types. They also travel along the toe of slopes between wetlands and uplands as well as tops of ridges and other contour related features. For these reasons, the movements of deer around their home ranges always have some sort of pattern. These patterns change with the seasons. Because deer movement patterns are not random, it is possible for a hunter to figure out, or "pattern," part of an individual buck's regular movements. The more that you know about a buck's movement patterns, the better will be your chances of seeing him.

If you really want to find out if a big buck is using an area, do a systematic search of the area for tracks, scrapes and rubs. Use Google Earth or other electronic mapping software either on your computer or GPS unit to study the terrain and landscape features. Set up your game cameras and don't forget to spend time in the field looking for deer. Walk and scout as much ground as possible. There is no substitute for quality time in the field.

Today's electronic technology is nothing short of fantastic. GPS units now allow you to instantly determine your precise location and see it plotted on a topographic map of the area. You can set way points and record tracks of your movements. When you return home or to deer camp, you can download all of this information to your computer where it can immediately be saved and displayed on electronic mapping and aerial imaging programs such as the free program Google Earth. With these computer programs you can view the landscape in three dimensions with resolution good enough in some areas to actually identify the tree that you stood under earlier in the day. You can then plan the best route to where you want to hunt and easily navigate to it even in the dark. You can plot or download scrape, rub and stand locations and save them for future reference. You can plot travel routes. If you track deer on snow, you can download your entire track from a day of tracking and see exactly where the buck you followed crossed the landscape.

Following the tracks of a buck is a guaranteed way of learning something about his travel patterns, feeding and bedding locations and general habits. The sky is the limit. What you are able to do with the equipment available today is limited only by your imagination.

Often, plotting information from scouting onto maps will suggest other locations that you may have missed and should scout later to complete the picture. If you observe carefully, you won't be able to help but learn about travel routes, home territories, and the habits of the deer in your area.

The ability to recognize and study the movement patterns of individual trophy bucks is certainly a critical step towards becoming a successful trophy buck hunter. The biggest bucks are by far the most difficult to observe. In fact, big bucks often live in areas having dense human populations, yet many may never be seen by a person. A radio tracking study of deer movement conducted in Texas provided a good example. A large buck was radio collared when he was 3 ½ years in an area having a relatively dense human population. For the following four years of his life, the big buck moved only at dawn, dusk and at night. He remained in extremely thick cover during the day and was believed to never have been seen by a person during the last four years of his life.

Just knowing that a large buck is in an area provides valuable information to a trophy hunter. Radio tracking data suggest that if you learn where a buck's primary bedding areas are that you will improve your chances of bagging him.

Still, there are no guarantees. That is why it is called hunting. That is why it will never be boring.

## Telling Buck Tracks from Doe Tracks

It is true that large deer tracks do not absolutely mean that they were made by a buck. There are always a few big does, although, they are never as big as the biggest bucks. It is also true that no shape or other measurable characteristic has been found to identify sex based solely on observation of a single hoof print.

Published scientific studies have suggested that does have smaller hoof length than bucks of equal weight. Although, the Trackometer was developed specifically for measurement of buck tracks, hoofs of does were also measured. I found no significant difference in maximum hoof width between equal weight bucks and does. So, the Trackometer can also be expected to accurately estimate the weight of does.

Even in northern states, most deer weighting in at over 130 pounds are bucks. Ten thousand adult does were weighed at check stations in Vermont during the archery and muzzle loader deer seasons of 2007 and 2008.

Among adult does in 2007 and 2008:

2 Doe in 1000 exceeded 160 lb.

9 Doe in 1000 exceeded 150 lb.

34 Doe in 1000 exceeded 140 lb.

114 Doe in 1000 exceeded 130 lb.

This means, if you measure a track with the TRACKOMETER and get a reading of 150 lb. or more, there is about a 99 % chance that the track was made by a buck. Even if you come across the track of a very large doe, following the tracks will soon reveal sign that will identify her sex if you pay close attention.

Does grow little after three years of age while bucks continue to grow until they are more than five years old. The energy drained by feeding fawns during summer uses up energy and nutrients that might otherwise be applied to growth.

I have often heard hunters talk about big "barren does." They usually believe that these are old and past their reproductive years. However, there may be other explanations. Does like females of other mammals can develop a corpus luteum cyst which secretes progesterone that signals the brain that the doe is pregnant. In response, the estrus cycle ceases. The doe will no longer come into heat or ovulate. Having no fawns to nurse, significantly more nutrients and energy are available to the doe for growth and weight gain. This may explain some of the big "barren doe" reports coming from hunters.

How many bucks are there weighing over 150 lbs? Obviously, this depends on where you are hunting. It depends on hunting pressure and the hunting regulations of the state you hunt in. The bottom line is: bucks have to live long enough to gain weight and grow mature antlers. States that shoot a large proportion of their 1 1/2 year old bucks won't have as many big bucks as states that don't crop off their young bucks.

Using my home state of Vermont as an example, the following table lists the number of bucks harvested per ten pound weight class during 2004 (the year before implementation of a forked antler restriction) and during 2010 (five years after implementation of the antler restriction).

| Field Dressed Weight (lbs.) | Number of Bucks 2004 | Number of Bucks 2010 |
|---|---|---|
| 80-89 | 109 | 12 |
| 90-99 | 431 | 116 |
| 100-109 | 1204 | 608 |
| 110-119 | 1534 | 1068 |
| 120-129 | 1426 | 1380 |
| 130-139 | 983 | 1360 |
| 140-149 | 637 | 1164 |
| 150-159 | 419 | 924 |
| 160-169 | 272 | 631 |
| 170=179 | 155 | 395 |
| 180-189 | 95 | 237 |
| 190-199 | 39 | 108 |
| 200-209 | 23 | 55 |
| 210-219 | 18 | 22 |
| 220-229 | 1 | 2 |
| 230-239 | 3 | 4 |
| 240-249 | 1 | 0 |
| No. Bucks =>150 lbs. | 1026 | 2378 |
| Total Harvest | 7350 | 8086 |

Notice that the forked antler restriction doubled the harvest of bucks weighing 150 lbs. or more. Before the antler restriction, about sixty five percent of Vermont's annual buck harvest was 1 1/2 year old bucks. This percentage dropped by a little more than half after the antler restriction. So, older bucks are bigger bucks. This shouldn't be any big surprise. Nearly 30 % of bucks taken in 2010 weighed 150 lbs. or more compared to just under 14% in 2004.

In 2004, 140 bucks out of 1000 weighed 150 lbs. or more compared to about 9 does out of 1000. Given these ratios, a track measuring 150 lbs. or more in Vermont in 2004 would have had nearly 16:1 odds of being a buck.

31

By 2010, 294 Vermont bucks out of 1000 weighed 150 lbs or more compared to about 9 does out of 1000. Given these ratios, a track measuring 150 lbs. or more in Vermont would have 33:1 odds of being a buck.

The antler restriction resulted is a big change. Vermont deer hunters love it. These numbers should give you a good idea of what you can learn by using tracks and the TRACKOMETER to scout for bucks.

During the rut, mature bucks tend to walk with a stiff-legged gate which results in dragging and an arcing of their feet outwards more than does and small bucks do. This trait can be observed from tracks especially when several inches of snow is on the ground. Bucks, particularly trophy size bucks, when walking leave staggered, spraddling tracks, that tend to toe out. This pattern seems to be caused by the massive width of their chests and greater amount of weight distributed onto the front legs, perhaps accentuated as the neck swells during the rut. Does and small bucks, on the other hand, step high and leave tracks that are more nearly in a straight line due to their relatively narrow body width and more even distribution of weight over the front and hind legs.

The massive, muscular build of big mature bucks makes them look almost short legged. When you see a large buck moving in the woods, his movements appear to be slower and more powerful than those of smaller bucks and doe. A good analogy might be made between the movement patterns of tackles and wide receivers on football teams. It is the differences in the build of the body and resultant way that the deer moves that leave the sign that indicates his size. Pay attention to the way deer behave as you watch them through the course of the year and to deer you see in hunting videos. You can learn a lot about the differences in body build and movement characteristics that are transcribed into the tracks of bucks.

**Wide spaced tracks are characteristic of heavy chested, wide body bucks. Bucks also tend to drag their feet. This characteristic becomes more pronounced during the rut.**

If you are observant, you will not follow a deer track very far before there will be signs that indicate a deer's sex. Bucks during the rut frequently stop to hook trees and brush and to make or freshen existing scrapes. When tracking a buck during the rut, it is usually not necessary to travel far before coming to a scrape or rub. I tracked a big buck all day on snow in Maine one year. He made two dozen scrapes and two dozen rubs during the course of the day. I was never far behind that buck, but I never caught up with him.

If the deer that you are tracking urinates, more clues to sex will be visible. Tracks of a doe will reveal that she has hunched back on her hind legs and urinated in her tracks leaving a wide spray pattern.

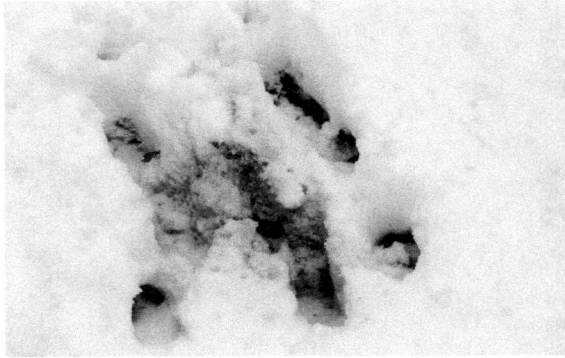

**Spray Pattern of doe urination.**

Bucks don't hunch back to urinate. If there is snow on the ground, there will be a round or key-hole shaped slot made by urine squirting straight down into the snow except when bucks rub urinate.

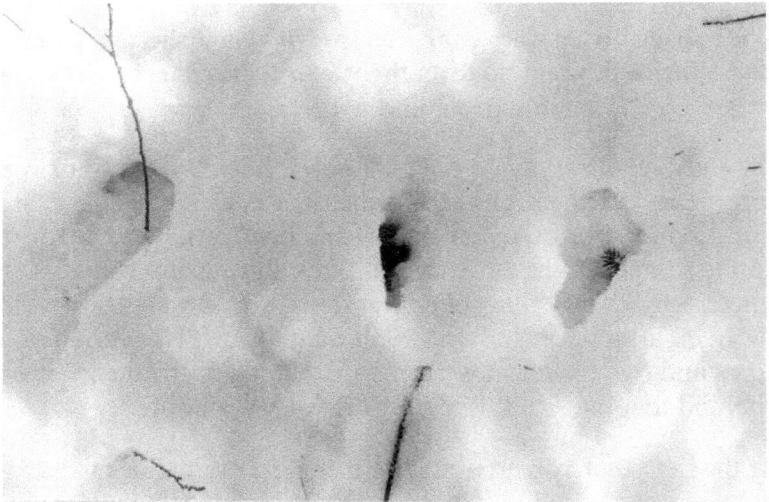

**When not rub urinating, bucks urinate straight down creating a hole or key hole shaped slot in the snow.**

Rutting bucks frequently rub urinate on their tarsal glands located on the inside of the hind legs. This also leaves a spray pattern of urine like does do. The difference is that the urine is usually dark colored, runs down the legs from the tarsal glands and drips or is flicked off the legs and hoofs as the buck walks away. As the rut proceeds, urine and tarsal glands become more darkly stained, progressing from yellowish brown to a dark coffee brown color and finally to almost black on some bucks.

When you come upon a deer's bed, you might get lucky enough to find the imprint of a buck's antlers in the snow. However, you almost always can find stains from a tarsal gland in the bed if it is made in snow. The tarsal gland from one of the hind legs is always imprinted in a deer's bed. The yellow to dark brown stain where the tarsal gland contacts the snow is unique to bucks. Even fawn bucks leave a pale yellow urine tarsal stains in their beds. I have never seen a urine stain from the tarsal gland in the bed of a doe.

Beds are also good places to find tracks of a deer. When a deer stands up from its bed, both front and rear hoofs are imprinted and easy to identify.

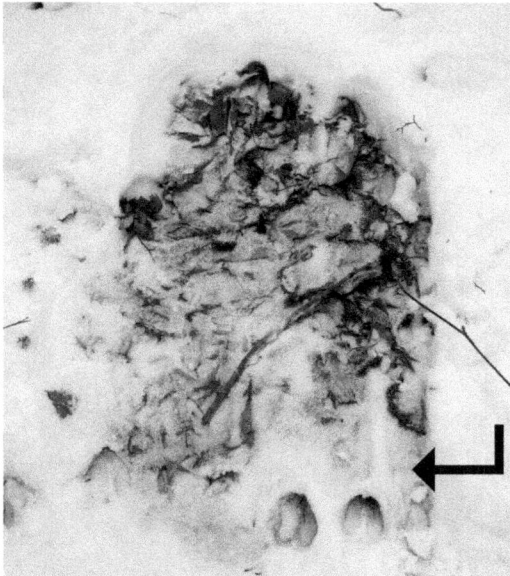

**Bed of a buck that laid on his right side leaving an imprint of the right rear leg in the lower right corner of this photo. The tarsal gland on the inside of the leg contacted the snow (at the tip of the arrow in the photograph) leaving a brown stain. Check out color images at www. trackometer.com. Rear hoof prints are clearly visible as they were made in wet snow when the buck stood up.**

Doe beds are typically found accompanied by the smaller, nearby beds of her fawns. Buck beds during the rut will be solitary unless a buck is tending a doe.

An experienced tracker will learn to recognize a variety of travel patterns peculiar to buck deer. For example, bucks typically skirt dense cover and choose the easiest walking. A buck in search of does; a buck pursuing a doe; bucks in a buck group: each behavior results in a trail of tracks having a pattern indicative of the behavior that the buck was engaged in. Plenty of clues also can be found as you follow deer tracks that reveal the deer's sex. Tracking is a detective game. It can sharpen the senses and greatly improve a hunter's observational skills.

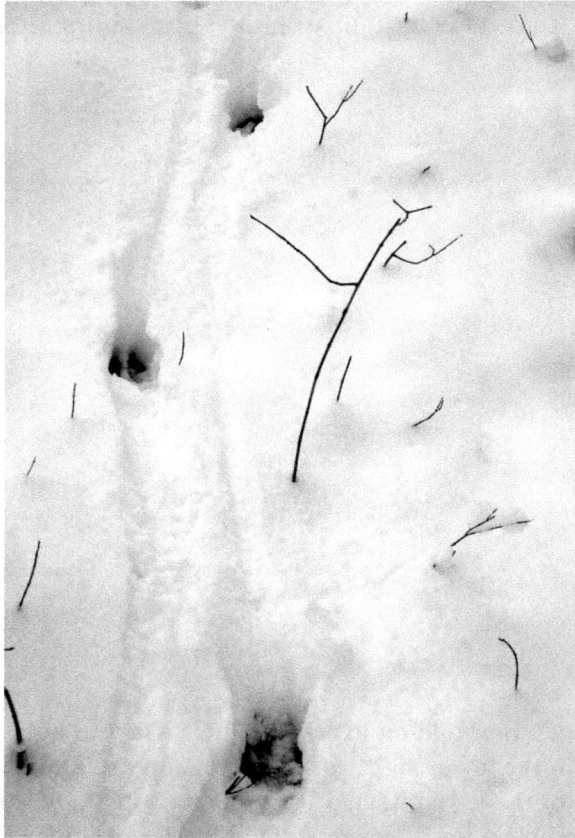

**Track of buck seeking does.**

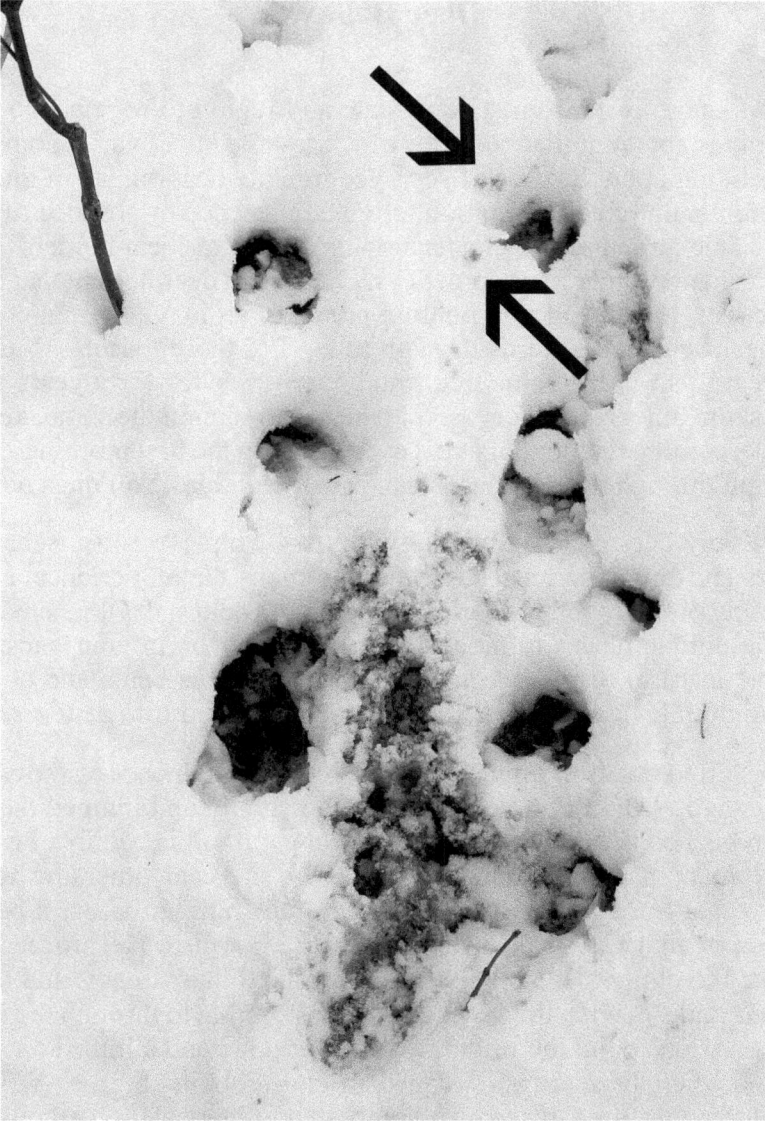

Urine drips or is flicked off the legs and hoofs of a buck as he walks away after rubbing and urinating on his tarsal glands.

# Deer Behavior

As one travels from state to state and region to region, it quickly becomes apparent that behavior of white-tailed deer varies somewhat depending upon the time of year, geographic location, lay of the land, the forest and field vegetation, climate, presence or absence of other big game animals, and the density and habits of local hunters. Long term changes in land use practices, changes in deer herd management practices, and changes in hunting practices all may result in changes in deer behavior patterns through time. For these reasons, you can't expect to sit in the same tree stand every year for forty years and at the same time expect deer travel patterns to remain the same, keeping bucks coming under your stand every year on the first morning of deer season through the decades. Change is inevitable. You must adapt.

Every deer is an individual with its' own personality, behavioral traits and life experiences. Some big bucks that experience a lot of hunting pressure may become pretty much nocturnal. Others may find some unique places to hide, for example, maybe in your back yard. Some learn to respond to other stressors such as bears and coyotes, agricultural and forestry activities and highway traffic patterns.

I started tracking a nice buck track on about 8 inches of snow a few years ago. I didn't move as quietly as I should and jumped the buck from his bed before I expected. He came out of his bed in a fast fluid movement that left no time for a shot. We saw each other and he soon knew that I was tracking him. I didn't track him far before it became apparent that this buck had been tracked before. He proceeded to make traveling miserable for me. He walked into streams and beaver ponds and stayed in the water as long as possible to through me off his track. At one point, he went into a beaver pond and climbed on a little island where he stood and treaded around watching for me. With few hunters in the area, it seems unlikely that hunters had given this buck the education that he used so well against me. It seems more likely that he had learned his lessons by being chased by coyotes. It seems to me that since the eastern coyote has arrived in New England that older bucks are more difficult to track.

On another hunt, I tracked a buck for four hours, over a mountain and into the valley below. Two to three miles after taking the track, I came upon a group of moose bedded right on the track that I was following. When moose scent a hunter in cases like this, they will generally get up and run noisily away. On the other hand, moose that see movement and don't scent a hunter will often get up and quietly move off. Knowing this and being down wind, I moved slowly and deliberately into the open so that the moose could see me. They got up and slowly moved off as I had hoped they would. I continued tracking the buck that had passed right between the beds of the moose. A few minutes later, I jumped and shot the buck as it ran from a nearby finger of woods where it had bedded after passing the moose.

**Buck that used moose as sentries.**

**Moose and deer interact with each other on a daily basis and use each other as sentries to guard against coyotes, humans and other predators.**

I have found that bucks seem to use moose as sentries or a means of hiding their track and scent trail. Again, I thing that harassment by the eastern coyote has lead to development of this behavior.

Behavioral flexibility, adaptability and variability are what keep deer alive. It makes hunting for whitetails a truly interesting and challenging sport.

Trophy deer hunters traveling from region to region to hunt must put in their time observing and schooling themselves on the local behavioral patterns of deer and adjusting their hunting methods to accommodate new situations. It is important to constantly be looking for new ways to find success.

# Home Range

If you plan to scout for bucks, you need to be familiar with the habits of deer in the part of the country where you will be scouting. You need to have a general idea of how big of an area a buck might be expected to occupy. You need to have a basic understanding of how deer may change their travel routes to and within feeding, bedding and wintering areas through the seasons of the year.

The area traveled year after year by a deer as it engages in its normal activities of feeding, resting, breeding, surviving winter and caring for fawns is known as the deer's home range. Tradition and habitat conditions together play a major role in the size, shape, and location of a deer's home range. Research has demonstrated that at least part of deer's home range is determined by learned experience. A good example is when fawns follow their mother to deer wintering areas each year. They learn the location of the wintering area and the area itself by spending there first winter there with their mother. Deer return to the same wintering area year after year as long as habitat conditions remain suitable. In this fashion, locations of wintering areas are passed by does from generation to generation.

In the case of a buck fawn, his home range may be partly learned from his mother during early life and partly modified by dispersal and association with other bucks. Aggressive behavior by does towards yearling offspring from the previous year occurs during June and July following birth of new fawns. Aggressive behavior by older bucks and does within his family group tends to further displace and modify the range of a yearling buck just prior to and during the rut. At the beginning of their second winter, young bucks join bachelor buck groups. Bucks congregate in loose groups through the course of the year except during the breeding season when they are most aggressive and have little tolerance for each other.

**Bucks congregate in social groups throughout the year, except during the rut.**

A deer's home range must be large enough to include all requirements for life and reproduction while being small enough to gain survival advantage through familiarity with the landscape. Home range familiarity provides survival advantages to a deer during its lifetime as it increases a deer's ability to successfully escape dogs, coyotes, wolves, bobcats, and other predators including hunters.

Typically, a deer's home range does not exceed two miles in diameter or about 3 square miles in area. Under certain conditions, home ranges may approach 10 square miles in area. Generally, a deer's home range tends to be more elongate than circular in shape probably because home range shape is often affected by the contours of the land which are defined by drainage basins and ridges which typically have strong linear shape components. By studying the movements of a group of deer in an area, it is possible to get a pretty good idea of the boundaries of their home range. The female descendents of a group of deer are likely to use roughly the same home range as their recent ancestors barring any major changes in the landscape, habitat or predator/hunting activity.

Home range size is known to vary with climate, season of the year, local diversity and mixture of forest and vegetation types, amount of

42

open versus forested area, population density of deer, and sex ratio. In cold, northern climates, home ranges of deer tend to be larger and less stable during the year than within warmer, southern climates. Seasonal shifts in behavior related to winter yarding, birth of fawns, and the rut cause deer to frequent greater or lesser portions of their home range at different times of the year. Deer living in habitats made up of large tracts of unbroken forests having uniform composition as well as deer living in areas with large expanses of flat, open fields or pasture tend to have the largest home ranges. Home ranges as large as nine square miles have been reported for some bucks in Texas where wide open spaces are abundant and water is limited at times.

Home range size is related to the distance deer must travel to find all of their daily and annual requirements for survival. Social pressures related to population density and sex also affect the home range size of a deer. As deer populations get larger, home ranges get smaller. Bucks tend to have larger home ranges than does. This is especially true during the rut when bucks tend to expand or shift use within their ranges.

Keeping in mind the average size of a buck's home range, you should be able to come up with a pretty good estimate of where bucks range in your own hunting area. By watching and photographing bucks, looking for tracks and learning the locations of feeding, bedding and wintering areas, you should be able to get a pretty good idea about where you will find members of one group of bucks and not another. Once again, the measurements that you can make with the TRACKOMETER can help you sort out the patterns you will find in the field and forest.

## Daily and Seasonal Activity Patterns

As you scout for deer, it is important to be aware of the daily and seasonal activity patterns of deer. Deer have predictable daily activity patterns. That does not mean that these patterns are always simple. There are seasonal patterns that recur at about the same time from year to year. There are daily patterns of activity that are similar from year to year at certain times of the year. Day length, moon light, temperature, wind, snow, food availability and even human activity

43

are factors that influence the activity patterns of deer through the seasons of the year.

In general, deer feed and travel most in the hours around dusk and dawn. Deer typically get up and feed about every five hours. Thus, deer will frequently be found feeding at about 11 a.m. as well as a couple of times during the night. Even so, some deer will tend to modify their schedules, particularly, if human disturbance is frequent.

As the breeding season approaches, activity in terms of miles traveled per day reaches its highest rate of the year. A major shift in activity occurs as buck groups break up. Aggressive behavior among bucks may displace some subordinate bucks from areas occupied during summer and early fall. Some will move tens of miles from their previous range. At this time of year, you may see bucks show up that have never been seen in the area before while others that you have watched all summer seem to disappear.

By observing deer, their tracks and other sign, you can monitor changes in deer activity patterns in your hunting area. A trail camera is also a useful tool for pinpointing the exact time of day a big buck is visiting a particular area.

## Bedding and Feeding Areas

Deer tend to bed in areas that provide the greatest comfort and security. They naturally want to be able to detect anything approaching while seeking security and comfort. If it is hot, they will head for slopes where a breeze and shade can be found. If it is cold, they will be found in softwood cover where a closed crown canopy keeps the forest floor warmer. During storms and high winds, deer are uncomfortable and seek shelter in thick cover, protected ravines, protected pockets, or leeward slopes. When weather and insects pose no particular discomfort, deer tend to bed in locations that provide security from predators and hunters. In hilly areas, deer often bed at higher elevation during the day where they can take advantage of a good view and thermal updrafts to sense animals approaching from below. At night they move down to lower elevations to feed and bed. Usually, breezes will move down the slope at night as the evening air cools down.  Deer again are in an advantageous position relative to the wind.

In flat country or low diversity habitats, where vegetation is of uniform size or composed of relatively few species of plants and trees, deer are more apt to bed in a core or central area within their home range.  When feeding, they tend to disperse out in all directions and then return to bed.  Home ranges of deer in these habitats are more circular than in hilly or diverse habitats.

Dense cover having concentrations of droppings during late summer and fall are generally bedding areas.  Bedding areas will be most concentrated when dense cover is most limited.  Knowing the location of bedding locations will prove valuable come hunting season.

Bucks like to bed on slopes, ridges or other promontories where they can see, smell and hear people or animals approaching.  Most of the year bucks run together in groups.  Bucks avoid positioning themselves where they are forced to look each other in the eye because staring is an aggressive behavior.  As a result, beds made by a group of bucks will typically be arranged in a fan-like pattern.  This behavior also helps the group maximize its' ability to detect approaching animals and people.

**Eye contact between bucks is an aggressive behavior.**

**Bucks bed in a pattern that avoids eye contact.**

If you locate several deer beds while scouting outside of the rut, use the TRACKOMETER to measure the tracks that you find in or near each bed. If you find only large tracks, exceeding the 140 lb. mark, you will almost certainly have found the beds of a buck group. Does bed with their fawns. Beds made by a doe/fawn family group will have small tracks in at least some of the beds. Fawn tracks are small. They will not register on the TRACKOMETER scale which begins at 90 lbs.

Learning where buck groups bed may come in handy when you are trying to locate a buck track during hunting season, placing tree stands or planning your access route to your tree stand so as not to spook bedded deer..

Through the course of the year, deer concentrate feeding activities in different areas of their home range in response to changing food availability. In early spring, deer congregate on south and east facing slopes which get more sunshine and produce green vegetation first. As spring and summer progress, the timing of growth, flowering, fruiting and ripening of the leaves, fruit and seeds of all kinds of plants proceeds at differing rates resulting in a great variety of food sources that are available in various locations at various times. When food is abundant and diverse, deer don't tend to concentrate. They wander around picking an choosing from a diverse menu. When drought or winter limits the availability and diversity of food sources, deer congregate in areas where food is most available.

Feeding areas are good places to look for tracks and observe deer while scouting. During the rut, bucks don't have feeding on their mind. That is not to say that they don't eat, they do. However, their trips to feeding areas are more likely to be in search of does than in search of food.

## Breeding Behavior (The Rut)

Little was known about the breeding behavior of white-tailed deer prior the mid-1970s. Since then, research has accelerated along with the interest in deer. Research in recent years has provided a wealth of new details describing deer behavior in general and rutting behavior in particular. Much of this information applies to deer throughout their range and is useful to whitetail hunters everywhere.

The daily and seasonal activities of bucks differ considerably from the activities of does. Except during the rut, bucks generally congregate in social groups (bachelor groups) of bucks only. On the other hand, does congregate in family groups that include her fawns of one or more years. As bucks approach the rut, behavioral differences between bucks and does become more pronounced.

Three stages of rutting behavior are now recognized. These are: the pre-rut, when bucks start marking their territories with rubs and scrapes; the rut, when the estrous of does is concentrated; and the post-rut, when most does have been bred but bucks have not re-assembled into their male social groups.

During the rut, bucks engage in three basic types of activities: seeking, chasing and tending. As the rut begins, bucks begin seeking does. They no longer tolerate other bucks. They are irritable and greatly increase their daily movements. They seek out doe groups and scent check them in search of a receptive doe. Rub and scrape making activity rapidly increases during this phase.

Chasing behavior begins about a week after seeking behavior begins. During this phase, some does are getting close to estrus. Bucks pursue these does which are not ready to stand for a buck. They repeatedly run a short distance then stop for the buck to catch up. Some physiological research suggests that this chasing behavior may release adrenaline which then causes other hormonal changes. These changes may hasten the onset of estrus thus shortening the time a buck spends chasing and tending a doe, increasing the available time for the buck to service others. Does frequently head for dense cover during this stage as they seek to elude the buck. During the chasing phase, fawns are driven off by the buck or left behind during the chase. Tracks tell the story, revealing a pattern of running, walking and standing tracks made by the pair. Sometimes more than one buck will be involved in the chase which may complicate the tracks.

The most active period of breeding begins about two weeks after bucks begin seeking does. A buck will tend a doe for 2 to 3 days. Then he will seek another doe, chase and tend her if he can. A buck tending a doe leaves a distinctive trail of tracks. When the buck and doe are walking, the buck trails directly behind her. This results in a unique trail that differs from the trails of does with fawns which parallel and frequently cross each other instead of following in line. The tending buck and doe bed close together. Following their trail, one will periodically find small areas that are all tracked up where they have bred.

The beginning of the rut changes the behavior of bucks as if a switch is has been thrown or a trigger pulled. The trigger is "set and pulled" by conditions of sun and moon light. Light plays a critical role in the breeding of white-tailed deer. The breeding season of whitetails is "set" in the fall in both the northern and southern hemispheres outside of the tropics. In the fall, the sun declines in the sky, shorting day length while the moon inclines in the sky, brightening moon light to a point where there is a sharp periodic change in how long each day the sun and moon together illuminate deer habitat. At the time of the new moon, days have the least illumination. While on the full moon, days have the greatest amount of illumination. Each of these events recurs on a 29 day cycle. There is no mere coincident that this matches the duration of the estrus cycle in whitetail does.

These changes in the daily light regime act as biological triggers resulting in activation of hormonal systems of deer. The pineal gland responds to light cues and mediates hormonal changes. These hormonal changes are responsible for all sexual changes in bucks, ovulation in does, as well as all of the behavioral characteristics exhibited by breeding whitetails.

The breeding season is most intense at higher latitudes where the difference between day length in summer and winter is greatest. The breeding season lengthens towards the equator.

North of the Mason-Dixon Line there exists the least amount of variation in the timing of the rut. It begins in October or November. In southern parts of North America, the rut can begin as early as September and as late as December depending on where you are on the continent. Much of this variability can be explained by variables that affect the timing and delivery of light stimuli such as differences in albedo and angular reflectance of light off water bodies. Some of it may also be genetic variability among the dozen or so whitetail subspecies in the southern U.S.

To learn more about the affects of the moon on the whitetail rut, get a copy of Deer and Deer Hunting Magazine's WHITETAIL CALENDAR. Since 1998, Charles J. Ahlsheimer and I have been preparing annual predictions of timing and progression of the rut published in the calendar.

## Buck Rubs

Bucks begin making rubs when they begin losing their velvet, mid-August through mid-September. Rubs made during this period are not as readily visible as rubs made during the rut because they generally occur in somewhat thicker cover where bucks have been bedding or feeding. These rubs don't seem to have the signpost function that rubs made during the rut have. Once velvet has been removed from antlers, rubbing activity declines sharply and doesn't pick back up until the pre-rut.

Rubs become increasingly visible and important as signposts as the peak of breeding approaches. They are aligned along a buck's primary travel routes which typically follow contours of the land and the edges of landscape features and habitat or forest types. The bulk of signpost rubs may be initiated by dominant bucks. However, other bucks may spot and also rub the tree previously rubbed by a dominant buck.

Does and young bucks attracted to rubs nibble, lick, and rub their foreheads against tubs. Rubs have clear social significance and are not randomly distributed, thus it is not surprising that research has found that rubs are usually found in the same area year after year. Remembering or recording locations where you find rubs is a good way to know where to go next year when you start scouting for the coming season.

An artificial rub can be made by rasping the bark from trees to attract bucks. Some hunter's use this technique along with application of deer scents or lures to attract or distract deer while hunting from stands or blinds. It is also a technique that you can use with your game cameras.

**Rubs on big trees in locations where they are highly visible are a sure sign that the rut has begun.**

Researchers from the University of Georgia have reported that bucks are very selective of the trees on which they make their rubs. They avoid trees with warty bark or low hanging branches. In the south, favored trees are black cherry, pine, and cedar trees, all of which produce strong aromas when the bark is rubbed off. My experience in northern forests suggests that alder, pin cherry, quaking aspen, tamarack, sumac, and willow are important rubbing trees in hardwood forests of the north. Cedar, balsam fir, and tamarack are commonly rubbed in the northern spruce-fir forests. It should be expected that tree species being rubbed will depend upon the species occurring in the area and the number of trees of suitable diameter that are available.

Most buck rubs are made on trees of ¾ to 3 ¼ inches in diameter. Large bucks tend to make rubs on larger trees, as large as 6 to 10 inches or more in diameter. A buck, typically, inserts a tree between the beams and rubs the tree near the base of the antlers so that the forehead contacts the wound on the tree.

The combination of odors from the forehead gland and those from the broken bark and sap of the tree produce a strong scent marker. The bright surface of the rub acts as a highly visible visual signpost to deer and is highly visible to hunters as well. Both bucks and does are attracted to buck rubs. Does have even been observed rubbing their vaginas as well as their heads against buck rubs although I have never seen any sign of this behavior while tracking deer.

Buck rubs are not necessarily limited to the activities of a single buck. Recent research has found that whitetail bucks are relatively tolerant of other bucks within their territory as long as they know their place in the social system. Social interactions among bucks within bachelor groups while antlers are still in velvet settle positions of dominance before the rut begins. Foot flailing rather than sparring with antlers is the aggressive behavior which decides social position. It may be that the most serious fights start during the rut when an unknown buck enters the territory of a dominant buck.

Buck rubs are a good place to observe tracks made by the front hoofs of a buck. Because a buck has to turn away from the tree to move on after making a rub, the tracks of the front hoofs are not overlaid by the tracks of the rear hoofs. Clear prints are often visible.

Even after trees grow in years following bark being torn by a buck rub, the healed scar remains visible for years. Scouting for old buck rubs during the summer can help you identify places where you should scout for new rubs in the fall.

**Old buck rubs from previous years provide evidence that bucks have used an area in the past and are likely to do so in the future.**

# Scrapes

Small scrapes may be found at most times of the year. However, scrapes associated with the rut begin being made in the fall as day length rapidly decreases. The intensity of scrape making activity reaches its peak during the two week period prior to the peak of breeding activity. Bucks make scrapes during this part of the rut while they are seeking and chasing does.

Scrapes made during the rut are typically made in areas having little undergrowth. They are frequently associated with small openings, old log roads, game trails, or other open, conspicuous sites. An overhanging branch is almost always found positioned over a scrape. This is called a "licking stick" or "licking branch." Licking sticks are generally positioned about 4 to 5 feet above the ground. They will invariably show signs of being chewed and sometimes hooked with the buck's antlers. Chewing, licking, rubbing the forehead and orbital gland at the corner of the eye on this stick leaves behind scent. Marking of the licking stick generally occurs just before the buck scrapes the ground with his front hoofs and rub urinates. During the scrape making process, bucks urinate on their tarsal glands located on the inside of each hind leg. As he rubs his legs together, urine mixes with pheromones and other secretions from this gland and runs down the buck's leg into the scrape leaving a strong odor.

Both scrapes and rubs tend to be localized within a buck's home range. Although scrapes and rubs occur in the same general areas, they aren't necessarily concentrated in the same areas. This may be related to differences in sites or habitat selected for rubs versus scrapes. Trees of a size and species selected for rubs simply may not be present in open areas or mature forests where scrapes are usually made. On the other hand, areas adjacent to old log roads and clearings that make good scrape sites frequently have good rub trees along their edges.

**Scrapes are almost always associated with an overhanging stick known as a "licking stick" on which scent is deposited. Bucks urinate on their tarsal glands during the scrape making process.**

Does are attracted to scrapes. They urinate in scrapes and leave strong scent trails that lead away from scrapes. Does that visit scrapes are easily followed by bucks that periodically check scrapes. The frequency with which a buck checks his scrapes may depend on the number of does in the immediate area. When many does are available per buck, bucks don't have to return to and check their scrapes very often.

Some hunters have speculated that a buck might service as many as 100 does per season. Does are receptive for about 26-30 hours. If a buck is tending a doe, he has no incentive to leave the doe to check scrapes or find another doe. Given that the primary breeding season is less than 21 days in length, it is a far more likely that a buck will have the time to tend fewer than seven and perhaps just three or four does during the primary rut. Does not bred during the primary rut cycle through estrus in about 28 day until bred or the light regime ends the cycle.

Just as artificial rubs have been found to attract deer, artificial scrapes made by biologists and hunters have also been proven to attract deer. Placement of sticks 4 to 5 feet above the ground in open areas where few branches are available at his height has been shown to lure bucks into making scrapes at these sites.

Hunters have been able to place artificial licking sticks that attract bucks. However, the success of this method must depend heavily upon the relative availability of overhanging branches. In a forest having an abundance of overhanging branches, artificial placement of one more branch is not likely to draw much attention. So, don't expect to go out and tack up a stick just anywhere and have a buck show up the next day to make a scrape.

Scrapes provide a great opportunity to observe and measure the tracks of a buck. Because bucks use their front hoofs to make the scrape, one or more front hoof tracks are frequently visible in a scrape. Often you can see the directional marks made by the scraping hoof. These can provide clues that will ensure that the track you find in a scrape is the track of the buck and not of a doe or small buck that has checked out the scrape and left tracks in it.

## Affects of Weather on Deer Behavior

It is no secret that deer respond to changes in weather. High winds, cold or hot temperatures, heavy rain and snow storms all influence the behavior of deer. In general, adverse conditions result in short term reductions in the movement of deer. Under adverse conditions, deer naturally seek shelter from the condition causing discomfort.

Deer deliberately move from exposed slopes to protected slopes in response to a cold wind blowing up hillsides. During high winds and heavy rain or snow, deer seek shelter in protected pockets, such as gullies, or in thick cover. These areas may be close at hand or require some traveling to reach depending on the diversity of habitat within a deer's home range. These protected areas will be used for shelter year after year, so pay attention when you find deer using these kinds of areas. If shelter habitat is in short supply within an area, the odds that deer will be using any given area increase. Shelter habitat where you have found evidence of bedding is a very good place to visit when the next storm hits during hunting season.

The affects of a storm are not always limited to the storm event itself. It has long been known that deer tend to increase or prolong feeding activities when barometric pressure is falling before a storm arrives. Increased activity may also follow a storm if high barometric pressure is accompanied by cold, sunny weather. On the other hand, deer activity may be greatly reduced for as many as 3 days following a heavy snow fall if weather remains unsettled.

When temperatures drop to very low levels, deer also tend to seek shelter. Research studies have correlated movement of deer to deer wintering habitat with both cold temperature conditions (mean daily temperature <20°F) and snow depth (>15-16 inches deep).

**When snow gets deep and temperatures get cold, deer move to areas having softwood cover where they find relief from the cold and easier walking.**

Just as the movement of hunters is hampered by deep snow, so is the movement of deer. Deer mobility declines sharply when snow depths exceed 10 inches and usually coincides with movement to lower parts of the deer's home range. Snow depth of greater than 16 inches, about knee deep, makes travel difficult for deer just as it does for hunters. Severe winter conditions for deer exist when snow is 18 inches or more in depth and/or air temperature is equal or greater than zero degrees. Wildlife biologists use these measures to estimate the relative severity of winter by counting the number of winter days during which either snow depth or air temperature reaches or exceeds the severe level.

# The Art of Tracking Deer

Old time western novels told stories of Indian and cowboy trackers who could successfully trail a coyote across solid rock in the dark with just a little light from the moon. Such stories made good reading and deer camp tales, but in reality, good ground conditions greatly improve the likelihood of successfully reaching the end of a buck track.

Tracking on bare ground is possible. It takes a patient, slow and methodical tracking even in cases where a faint blood trail is present. Deer scuff up and turn over leaves as they walk or run. Leaves are often damp on their underside. As a result, turned over leaves appear as darker colored leaves that provide a visible a trail that can be followed. However, it usually doesn't take long before leaves start drying and causing the trail to fade away especially if there is a breeze. Berry bushes, shrubs and grass also reveal trails and direction of travel. Look for smaller stems that have been pushed in the direction of travel and then hung up against larger stems when they snap back into place. These reveal the direction of travel.

Tracking deer borders on impossible when tracks of many other deer cross or intermingle with those of your quarry unless the buck you are tracking is a lot bigger than other deer in the area. When I find a really big buck track on bare ground, I give tracking a try. As they say, nothing ventured, nothing gained.

The TRACKOMETER can be a big help in these situations because it provides an objective way of telling tracks apart. Measurements made with the TRACKOMETER as well as other characteristics of your buck's tracks can make the difference between staying on or losing the track.

Besides the difficulties involved in reading sign on bare ground, noise made while tracking tends to be louder, more frequent, and carry farther than when an insulating layer of snow covers the ground. Sound also seems to carry farther on cold, dry days. For these reasons, it is much easier for a deer to locate and stay ahead of a tracker on bare, dry ground than when snow covers the ground and vegetation. Adding to hunting difficulty is the fact that it is harder to spot deer when there is no snow on the ground to provide improved contrast between the colors of deer and forest.

Ideal tracking conditions exist when 4 to 16 inches of soft snow cover the ground. Under these conditions, tracks are easy to follow while movements of the tracker are muffled yet relatively unhampered by snow depth. More snow does not always mean better tracking. Once snow depth reaches knee level, walking becomes an effort and tracking becomes hard, tiring work. Deer tracks can be easily followed in one to 4 inches of snow, however, the sounds of twigs and branches breaking underfoot are not as muffled as they are when snow is deeper. Some hunters won't track on crusty snow because it is noisy. The crunching noise made while walking on crusty snow seems extremely noisy to the ears of a hunter. However, I am not convinced that the sound carries very well. I have successfully tracked bucks on crusted snow. I have also noticed that other hunters have to be pretty close before they can be heard. Perhaps, sounds are muffled at a distance by the snow covered landscape. I don't let snow condition deter me from a day of tracking.

Tracking in areas where there are a lot of other hunters can be frustrating if you don't have patience. It is common for other hunters to knowingly or unknowingly cut ahead on a track that another hunter is following. Don't just give up when you see that another hunter has cut ahead on your track. The average hunter does not track a deer very far before giving up. Some of the best tracking conditions occur during storms when many hunters desert the woods for the warm and dry refuge of deer camp. So, getting on a track whenever you find an opportunity and being persistent will eventually pay off.

How do you learn to track? Experience is the answer! Learning to track from a tree stand is kind of like learning how to dance by watching from a bar stool. It just won't work. You have to get out there and step on some toes and twigs.

You can't develop woodsmanship or orienteering skills sitting in a tree stand. You can't learn how to move quietly through the woods from a tree stand. And, there is only so much that you can learn about deer behavior from a tree stand.

If all the lands around your hunting area are posted, you may not have room to use tracking as a deer hunting method. But, even if the properties that you hunt are not large enough or don't provide opportunities for a big country tracking experience during deer season, you may still find opportunities in the off-seasons to learn tracking skills while scouting for deer.

The fastest way to scout for and learn about the presence, behavior, and movement patterns of white-tailed deer is by observing tracks and tracking deer. Tell-tale signs of feeding, bedding, breeding, and movement patterns can be read from the ground and vegetation by an observant tracker. This makes tracking a great scouting technique. Scouting for deer can provide you with year around enjoyment.

In northern regions where snowfall regularly occurs during hunting season and hunting pressure is not as great as in some areas, tracking deer in the mountains and big country where large paper company or public land ownerships provide plenty of room to travel is an effective and commonly used hunting method. Hunting days that include or follow a good snowfall invariably result in a busy day for deer check stations. For the hunter interested in bagging a trophy buck, tracking is one of the most productive methods by which a hunter can scout the movements of and hunt for a specific trophy animal.

Pre-season scouting and knowledge of behavior patterns from past hunting seasons can give a hunter an edge and greatly improve the odds of locating a buck, especially a buck that has learned to successfully avoid hunters by adopting nocturnal habitats. Under ideal snow and weather conditions, tracking may provide the best chance of taking a buck. The more a hunter observes and learns about the details of deer behavior, the greater will grow his or her appreciation and enjoyment of hunting and scouting.

Don't expect anyone to ever tell you everything that there is to know about tracking deer or shooting a trophy buck. I doubt that anyone knows or will ever know it all.

Luck may play some part in the earliest hunting experience of the novice or first week-end hunter who spends only a few days in the woods each fall. In fact, if it were not for luck being involved in the taking of his first deer, many whitetail hunters might well have become discouraged and quit hunting before ever developing basic hunting skills.

Regardless of whether you are a still hunter, an ambush hunter, a tracker, a track runner, a driver, a scrape hunter, a brush buster, or if you use lures or calls to hunt deer, the ability to locate deer sign and the home territory of a trophy buck is essential to every hunter who hopes to become consistently successful. The development of hunting skills reduces dependency on luck and builds a set of skills that you can enjoy and be proud of.

Consistent hunting success depends on much more than a little luck. It takes time in the field and attention to detail to develop the skills and attitude of a good hunter. The skills bring lasting satisfaction and pleasure that go far beyond the act of killing a buck.

## Locating and Identifying a Buck Track

You wake up at home or at deer camp to find that it has snowed six inches during the night: snow tracking conditions are perfect. What now? Where are you going to find that big buck track? Do you have a plan? Yes, you should already have a plan.

Actually, you should have a number of alternate plans all worked out based on pre-season scouting and past years of experience. Your pre-season scouting should provide you with a list of places that deer cross roads or trails that you can check for fresh tracks even before shooting hours arrive. If the storm has been accompanied by high winds that wipe away tracks, you may want to check locations that provide shelter from wind and snow and any places where you have come across deer beds or bedded deer following storms in the past. You can also check ridge tops where deer may have crossed a divide to get to the wind protected side of a hill or mountain. On the lee side of the hill or mountain, the wind may not have erased all of the tracks.

Ideally, the first thing in the morning, you will find a good buck track made just before daylight. If it is before or after the rut, odds are good that the buck will have fed before or at first light and then bedded nearby. If snow is still falling at or near daylight and you have a fresh track, there is a very good chance that the buck is very close by.

Deer tend to lay down shortly after sunrise, so slow down, stop and think. Your best chance of taking a buck is if you can catch him in or getting up from his bed the first time. So, it is not wise to go galloping off on the trail making a lot of noise.

The first thing that you want to do is figure out if the track you have found was made by a buck that you want to spend time tracking. Use the TRACKOMETER if you are not sure of size, and remember the characteristics which distinguish buck tracks from doe tracks. Follow the tracks a ways to make sure you know how big the deer is and if it is a buck. Look for sign that will tell you whether he is feeding, looking for a place to bed, or looking for a doe. Answer the question: are the tracks fresh?

If you decide to take the track, quietly get your gear together, slowly and deliberately take the track. Be patient and keep your eyes looking for deer. It is not uncommon to find that a buck has bedded just a short distance from a road or other spot where you first take the track. So, don't slam your truck door.

## Aging Tracks

**Tracks at first light are obviously fresh after snow has fallen during the night.**

In the case of waking up to a new snowfall, it is pretty easy to tell how old tracks are. Even deer tracks that appear as dimples in the snow, may be fresh enough to permit the tracker to quickly come upon the deer in his bed as long as you make sure you know which direction the tracks are headed. When snow is deep and powdery, it is sometimes hard to tell which way a buck went. Following a track in the wrong direction won't make your day, so spend the time to be sure of the tracks direction.

Estimating the age of tracks is detective work. It is a matter of keeping a time line of events that have happened in the past hours and days. Knowing the times that events have occurred provides context which you can use to estimate the timing of other events such as the time that a deer crossed a road.

For a simple example, if you heard a snow plow go down the road at 5 a.m. then you go out and observe a fresh set of deer tracks crossing the plowed road at 6 a.m., the track is obviously less than an hour old. Similarly, if you know that it rained during the night and you find a sharp, uneroded track in the morning, you know that the track was made after it stopped raining. Use a calendar or waterproof notebook to keep track of events. Pictures also can be a big help.

The rates at which tracks age are complicated by weather and other conditions that are not necessarily simple. Getting good at aging tracks is mostly a matter of careful observation and experience.

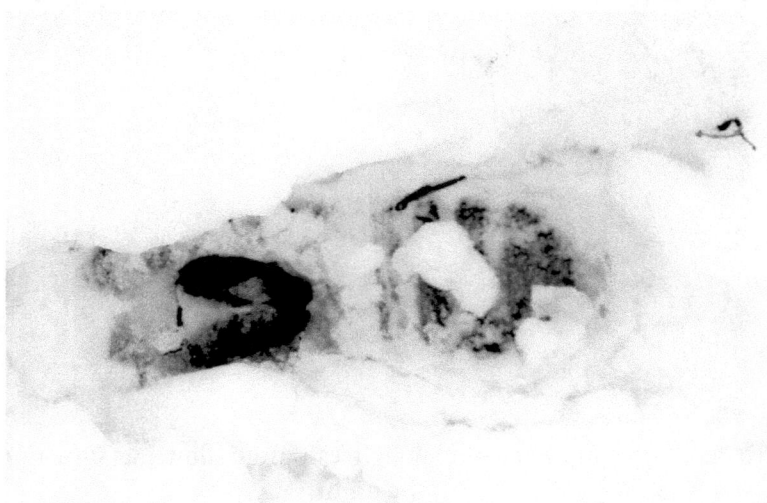

**A deer track in your own boot tracks can tell you a lot about when the track was made.**

**Tracks that appear as mere dimples in the snow can be less than an hour old when it is snowing hard.**

If you go to deer camp or even if you hunt from home, it pays to get into the field several days before you start hunting. Scout and begin recording, in your mind if not on paper, when it rained, snowed, froze, thawed, blew a gale, turned sunny, and any other condition that affects the eroding, covering, drying, freezing, thawing and anything else that affects the decay and aging of tracks.

The drying rate of soil cast from a fresh track provides clues to the age of the track. Sun or wind dry soil. When did this happen?

This track shows no evidence of drying.

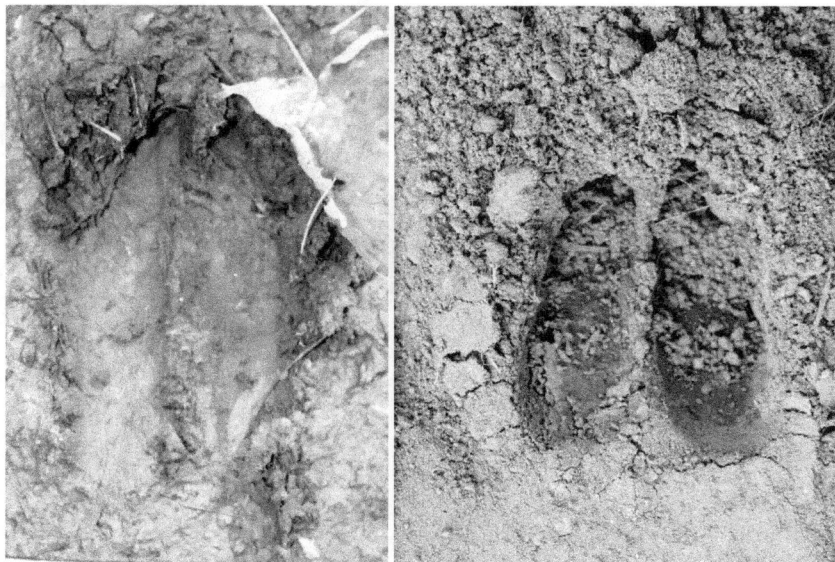

**Tracks dry out, erode or get filled in through time.**

**Tracks in advanced stages of weathering and aging.**

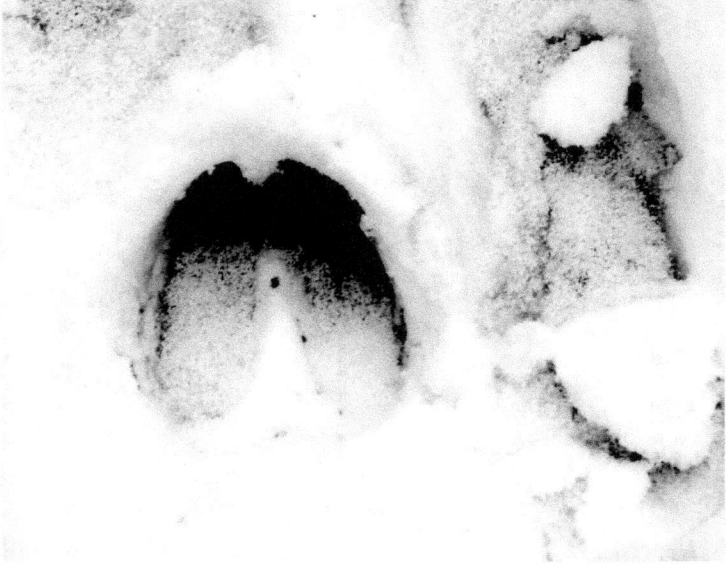

**If you know when and how hard it has snowed at known times in the past, a dusting of snow in a track can tell you when the track was made.**

The key to aging tracks is to understand the conditions that cause tracks to age and to then keep track of events that result in conditions that cause aging to occur. Rates of aging depend on many factors that could be scientifically quantified, however, most trackers use their experience and judgement to make on the spot estimates of a tracks age.

The ability to recognize conditions that result in aging of tracks will help you place in context the sequence and relative timing of events that could affect the aging of tracks and other deer sign in your hunting area. This knowledge will form the bases of your ability to accurately age deer tracks and sign.

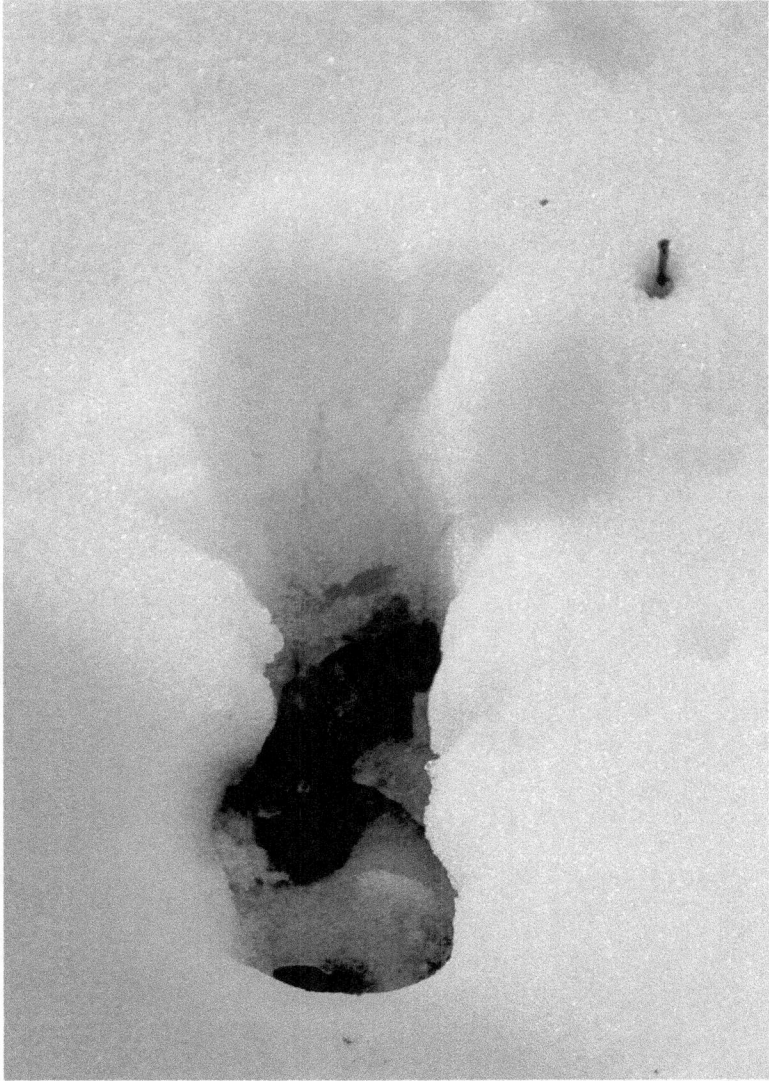

**Buck track made in wet snow.**

Tracks made in wet snow have soft margins instead of the sharp edges found in tracks made in crusted snow.

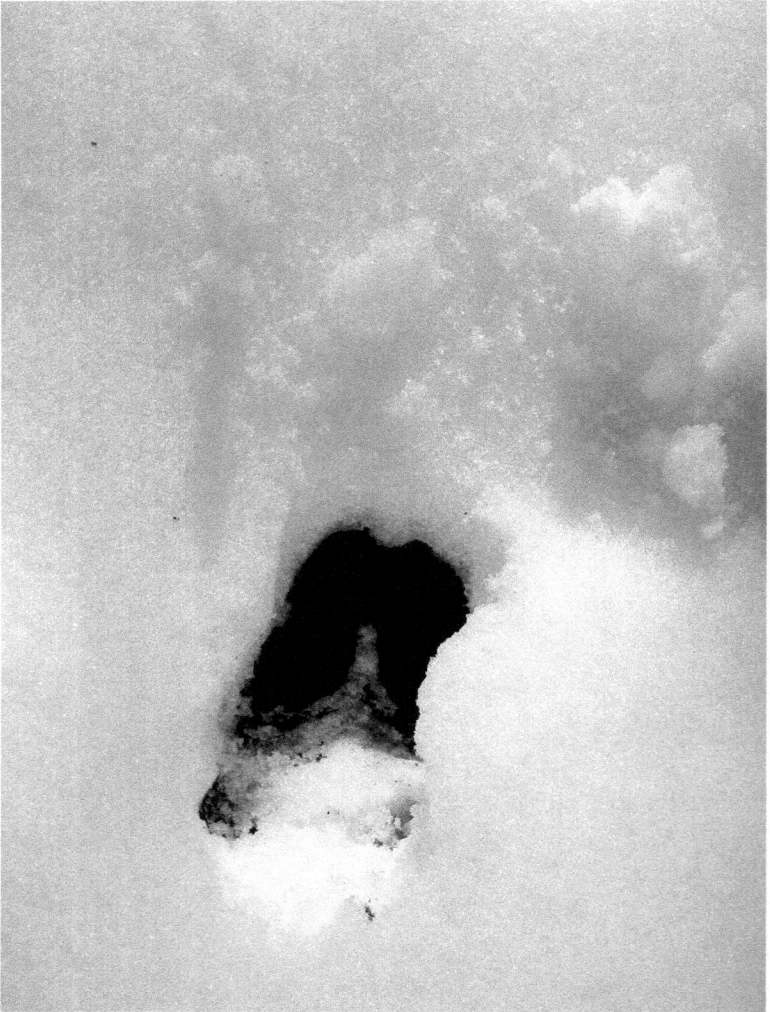

**Buck track made in crusted snow has sharp edges and fragmented, granular cast off in the direction of travel.**

It is important to recognize the differences in tracks made under various snow conditions. Knowing when warm or cold conditions resulted in wet or crusted snow provides clues to the age of tracks.

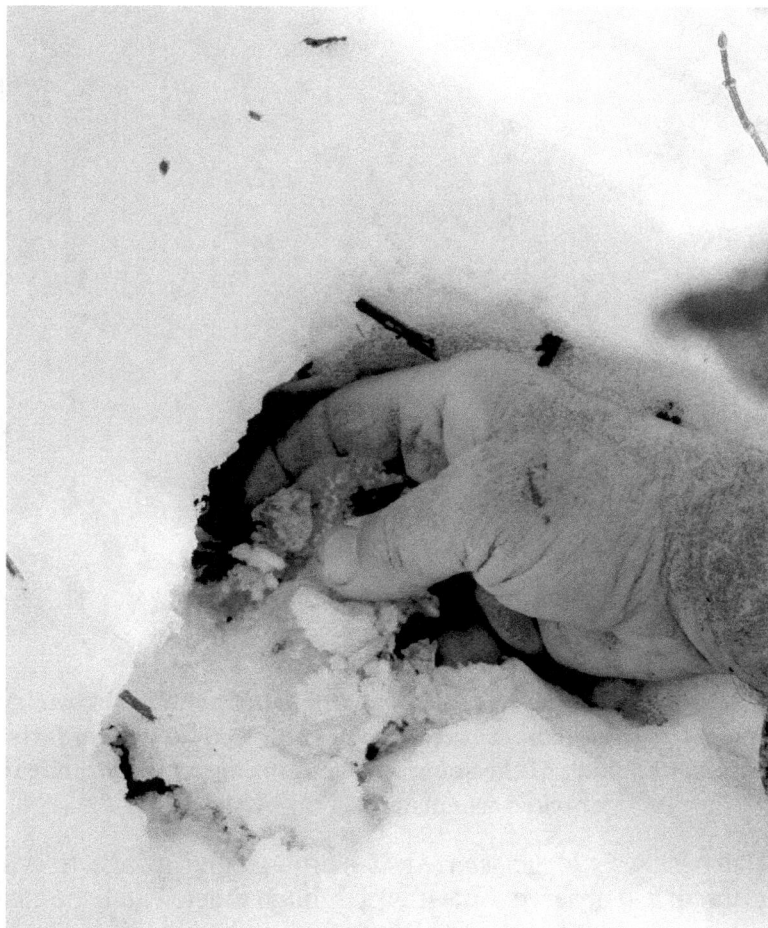

**Check for ice in the bottom of tracks made in wet snow to make sure that they have not frozen and thawed.**

Wet snow will often freeze at night and thaw again the next morning. Tracks made the previous day when the snow was wet may look like fresh tracks made after the snow has softened again the next day. If there is ice in the bottom of the track, the track was made the day before.

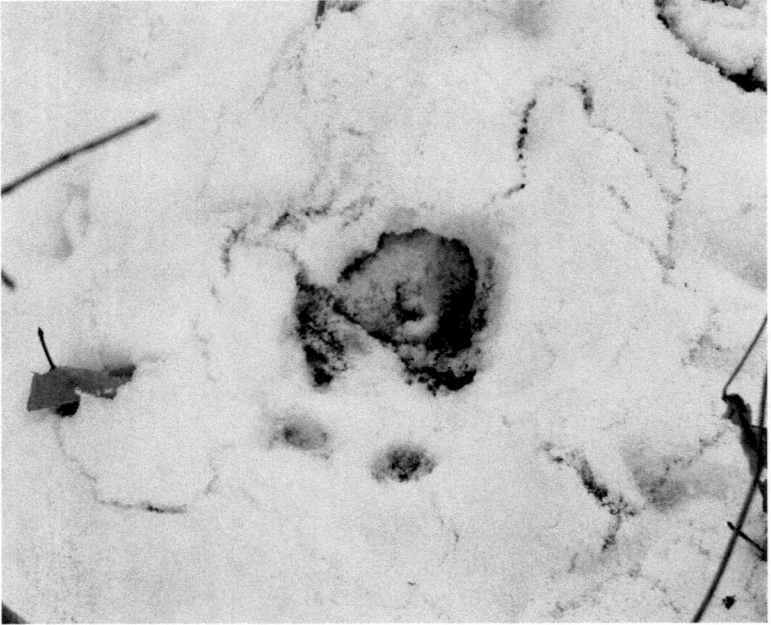

**Powder snow fell on wet leaves the morning before this track was made. Freezing temperatures the next night froze the underlying leaves. Cracking of the snow occurred because the frozen leaves cracked when stepped on by the deer.**

The best way to get started at learning how to age tracks is to experiment and observe some tracks through time. Watch the changing condition of sets of tracks made at a known time with different weather conditions. A simple way to do this is to make some tracks of your own and watch how they change. Check them later and keep track of the elapsed time.

I did this myself a few days ago. I have noticed many times while tracking deer that sometimes fresh tracks will still have murky water in them. This murky water is caused by silt or clay particles that are suspended in the water. I wondered just how long it takes for the water to clear up. So, I went out and made some tracks in puddles and timed the settling rate or time that it took for the water to clear.

In one case, it took only 15 minutes. In another case, it took 35 minutes. Why the difference? Soil particles are scientifically classified as clay, silt, sand or gravel. Clay particles are the smallest followed by silt. In still water, the smallest sand particles settle out in just about 60 seconds while the smallest silt particle take about 12 hours. There is a whole law (Stoke's Law) that describes how fast particles of different sizes settle out. So, if you were a crime scene investigator you could really go to town applying science to determine how far a deer was ahead of you.

Yes, that would be a little impractical given the time it would take would provide your buck plenty of time to reach the next county. But, the point is that there are real world differences in simple things such as how fast murky water clears up. These, in fact, can be complex in nature and might require detailed scientific analysis to fully understand. Such analyses could conceivably tell you down to the second how long it has been since a deer stepped in a puddle and stirred up the mud. Even if it may be impractical to apply in the field, science can be used describe and explain the processes of aging tracks.

Fortunately, humans have an amazing computer under their hunting hats. A hunter can use observation, experience and knowledge in a learning process that provides an incredible ability to judge conditions and estimate the age of deer tracks and other sign in the field without scientific measurement and testing. This is the art that one has to develop through practice to become a good tracker.

Under dry conditions tracks may look fresh for a long time. When it is snowing hard, a set of tracks only minutes old may look as "old as the hills." Are the tracks frozen? How long should it take for them to freeze at the current air temperature? Has it rained on the tracks? Have the tracks thawed and been refrozen? Have other animals crossed the track you are following? Does the track you are following cross older tracks that you have seen earlier?

The art of determining the age of tracks requires an ability to observe conditions of a track and relate these conditions to the timing of other known events. It is necessary to pay attention to details. To get good at aging tracks, you must make a conscious effort to develop your observational skills and spend time in the field practicing.

Determining which direction a set of tracks is headed is also critical to tracking success. Sometimes this is simple and sometimes it is not. There have been a lot of chuckles around camp fires at the expense of novices who have unknowingly tracked deer backwards. As snow depths increase, difficulty in determining the direction in which the deer is traveling increases, especially in dry powdery snow. Often it is all but impossible to find a track that has a visible outline of a hoof print. Tracks may sometimes appear to be just scuff marks.

A number of clues help the observant tracker determine the direction of travel in these situations. If the track passes over ground that is soft under the snow, the outline of hoof prints may be revealed by brushing away the snow or running your fingers down into the track to feel the imprint in the surface below. Careful examination of the edges of the slots where the hoofs have gone in and come out of the snow will generally indicate a spray or "cast-off" pattern that has been made as the deer's feet were pulled from the track slots. This spray pattern of snow or soil will extend away from the slots in the direction of travel.

A smooth, rounded margin occurs at the narrower end of a slot where the hoof enters the snow. A more irregular margin with cast off snow occurs at the other end of a slot made as the feet are pulled of the track and explode out of the snow. The wider end of these "key hole" shaped slots points in the direction of travel. This key hole pattern may be recognizable even in tracks that have been nearly snowed in.

**Note the wider offset and arching drag marks of buck track on right.**

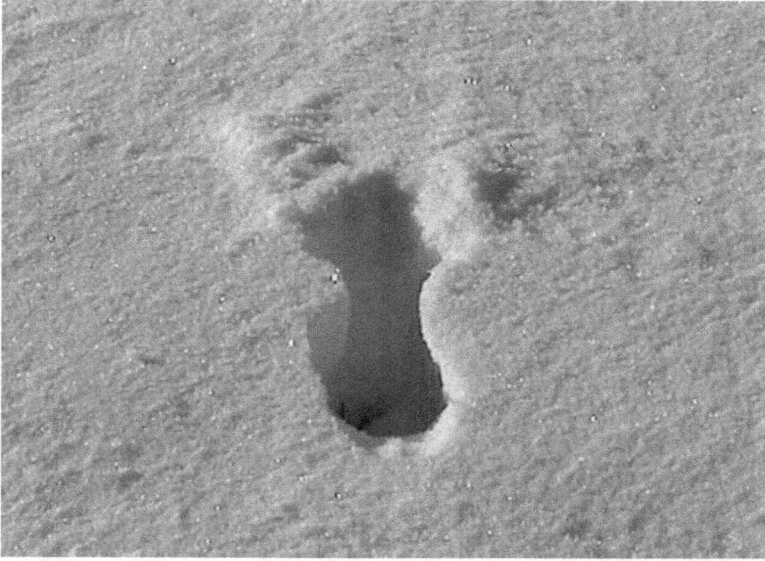

**Snow is cast in the direction that the deer traveled. Keyhole like track slots have a wider end that points in the direction of travel.**

If the buck you are tracking has made a rub, the side of the tree on which bark remains almost always marks the direction in which the buck has traveled. The side of the tree approached by the buck will be the side rubbed clean of bark.

As a general rule, a buck is most likely to keep going in about the same direction that he was headed in when he approached the tree. Observing, knowing and remembering little things like this can give you an edge when tracking.

## Taking the Track

When setting off on a track, again, remember to go slow! I can't tell you or myself too many times, go slow. The good news is: when undisturbed, mature bucks tend to take the easy way. This makes the trek easier for the tracker. Bucks tend to avoid thick brush and deep snow. They tend to follow the contours of the land. When tracking a buck and losing the track, it is wise to assume that a buck continued in the same direction of travel until the time that you find clear evidence that he has changed course. I have found traveling through the woods often follows an easier path when I am on a buck track than when I am navigating on my own.

**Bucks tend to avoid brush and other objects that make walking difficult.**

Concentrate every instant on moving soundlessly. You won't succeed at this. You will always make some noise. Still you need to relentlessly pursue this goal. Maintain control of your body, your balance, at all times and test your footing carefully, toe first, to feel branches that might crack underfoot. You should be wearing boots with soft soles that allow you to feel branches under foot. Plant every step with care to avoid slips and falls. Move every branch carefully aside with your hands or arms so that they don't make scraping sounds against your clothing or gun. When moving your hands or turning your head or upper body, do this slowly and smoothly. Move your eyes as much as possible and minimize turning of your head and upper body. When you can do all of these things simultaneously while making only fleeting glances at the ground to stay on the track, you will be getting good.

I have had days when I have been a good tracker. I have had a lot more days when I wasn't. The biggest challenge is to keep your head in the game, to be able to concentrate and execute these things without any words, music or thoughts running through your head to distract you. The over use of radios, GPS units and compasses can result in unnecessary distractions. Use these gadgets strategically. There is plenty of time to play with them and talk to your buddies at home in the off season. Pay attention to the tracking.

Try not to walk directly in tracks that you are following. You may need to back track and take another look at them. You may also find out too late that a buck has back tracked or that another deer track has intermingled with the track that you are following. It can get pretty hard to sort out tracks and find where a buck has back tracked and veered off if you have covered the deer tracks up with your own tracks.

You must see a buck in order to shoot a buck! You can't see a buck if your eyes are glued on his tracks. Don't stare at the tracks. It isn't necessary but is a natural tendency. If you don't break yourself of this habit, the most you are likely to see is a tail disappearing into the distance. Just glance at tracks briefly while you are moving. It is easier to notice movement of a deer when you are standing still than it is when you yourself are moving. So, stop frequently. The best time to take a closer look at the tracks is while standing still. Use of a small pair of binoculars to scan ahead for deer when you come upon spots that afford good views will increase your chances of spotting a buck.

Stop after every few steps. Try to sound like a walking deer. When possible, try to stop next to a tree, bush, or below a ridge line to help mask your movements and body outline from any deer that might be watching. When you have a good vantage point, scanning ahead with your binoculars will often pay off by turning up an ear, antler, or eyeball that you might have otherwise missed. Don't stop where the sun will glare in your eyes. You won't be able to see very well. If you have to travel into the sun, stop behind trees or other objects so that your eyes will be shaded when you look around for the deer. A cap having a visor will also help shade your eyes. Stop before topping a ridge line or entering a clearing or clear-cut. Use cover to peek over the ridge or into the opening and check for deer before moving forward. You want to see the deer before they see you.

After you have satisfied yourself that the deer is not in view, you can take another look at the tracks. Follow the tracks with your eyes as far as you can see them and try to locate a landmark in their path as far out as you can see. Once you know where the track is headed, move forward in the direction of your landmark, looking for the deer and not at the track. When you reach the spot that you marked, take a good look around for deer. Then move on and repeat this process over and over as you move along the track. Be patient, this is not as easy to do as it sounds. It is easy to get in a hurry and start moving faster than you should. You must keep telling yourself to slow down.

A tracker should spend 80 to 90% of his visual effort looking for a piece of a deer. Train your eyes to first take in a wide view. Try seeing the landscape as a whole. Let your eyes naturally pick out things that look out of place. With practice, you should naturally come to recognize objects that have been disturbed or seem out of place. Pay attention to any movement at the fringes of your view where peripheral vision is most sensitive to movement while at the same time trying to focus on the outer limits of your forward view.

**Train your eyes to instantly recognize patterns**

Looking for distant objects first is important because a deer in the distance generally can move out of sight much faster than a deer that is closer. Once satisfied that nothing is moving near the limits of your view, look over the landscape closer to you. Carefully inspect any horizontal outline that might be the outline of a deer's back; any vertical profile that is colored like a deer's leg; and any visual pattern that looks like the ears of a deer looking at you. Trees are oriented vertically. Any horizontal outline should get special attention. Deer legs have a vertically oriented pattern of shading. Dark hair on the front and light hair on back of legs makes a pattern of contrast that can help a hunter distinguish deer legs from trees. Look for the distinctive pattern of a deer's head and ears looking alertly in your direction. Training your eyes to see deer by watching deer in the off season will greatly improve your ability to spot deer while hunting.

When watching deer in the off season, think about the elements of the deer's image that make it stand out from the forest or field. Practice using these patterns to locate deer until you use them without conscious thought.

Concentration while hunting is one of your most important skills. It marks the difference between and expert and a novice. Your mind must be thinking only about hunting. You must not think about work, your wife, and let music run through your mind, or in any way distract yourself from the task of tracking and spotting deer. This is a skill that you have to work on to develop. It will be refreshing if you can master it. It is not easy.

When you do see a deer, do yourself and us all a favor and make sure of your target. Train yourself to be aware of and use your peripheral vision to locate trees, logs, or other objects that can be used as shooting rests. Taking the time to get a solid shooting position will greatly improve your accuracy and success in getting good clean kills. You often have a lot more time than you think to make a shot. Deer are curious. They often stop to look back at a tracker, presenting a standing shot. Don't be upset if the deer doesn't stop. As long as you haven't scared him out of his wits with a barrage of bullets, nine times out of ten he will soon slow down and you may get another chance. Waiting ten to twenty minutes before following a deer provides a good chance that the deer will forget that you were ever around. So, be patient and take your time.

After satisfying yourself that no deer are in the distance, inspect your immediate surroundings. Don't forget to look behind you. It is not unusual for a buck to circle around and bed overlooking his track. Bucks will often lay still in their beds while a hunter passes and then get up and move away behind the hunter.

Undisturbed deer tend to travel into the wind especially in heavy cover where the distance a buck can see is more limited. Deer are able to travel with the wind in their face almost constantly by tacking at various angles into the wind. This lets them smell anything that is ahead of them. This trait provides an advantage to a tracker who will rarely be detected by a deer's keen nose when he is on the track. On the other hand, a tracker will often be able to smell deer for the same reason. I have noticed that the instant a gust of wind first strikes my face is the instant when I catch the strongest scent of a deer. It seems as if the scent rides on the front of the wind. Learn what deer smell like. When you smell deer, be alert.

Deer in meadows, clearings or open woodlands where they can see long distances may travel in any direction regardless of wind direction. When running, deer also seem to move down or cross wind. In these situations, I believe that deer are relying primarily on their eye-sight When deer can't see very far, they have to rely on their nose and ears. It makes sense that they would want to position themselves to use these senses to best advantage.

Deer behave differently depending on the wind. On cool, moist days without wind, scent doesn't seem to disperse or travel much. On either snow or bare ground, a quiet tracker or stalker is able to get surprisingly close to deer without being detected. I have had a buck walk up to me in the forest to within arms length and neither see or smell me. I could see from the look in his eyes that he couldn't tell me from a tree even though I was not standing behind cover. If the air and wind conditions had been different, this never would happen.

Deer seem to become nervous and spooky when wind speeds exceed 10 miles per hour. At slower wind speeds deer seem to have little trouble using sent to detect and locate the position of a hunter. It seems likely that when winds become gusty and exceed 10 miles per hour that deer can detect the hunter but may have greater difficulty telling where a hunter is. They seem to have to rely more on their eyes and ears than their nose when the wind blows hard.

As wind speed increases, I have noticed that the tendency of deer to move into the wind diminishes. In open woods or clearings where deer can see well, they may travel in any direction. They use their eyes and ears which provide longer range threat detection than their nose.

I have tracked bucks many times under light wind conditions for an entire day at a time with the wind always in my face while sometimes making in an entire circle. When winds are light, the breeze seems to follow the contours of the land rather than sticking to the direction of the prevailing wind and may swirl around a basin or valley. I have also tracked into the wind along ridges that ended. At the end of the ridge, bucks have a tendency to run when the wind direction abruptly changes while they are traveling. They may run, relying more on eyes and ears until they head into the wind moving along a new contour of the land.

It would be nice if some of the folks who conduct radio tracking studies would take the time to investigate the micro-level effects of wind on the movement patterns of deer. Today's technology makes it possible and practical to approach real time tracking of wildlife.

When the wind blows a gale, deer head for cover often on the lee side of a mountain, in gullies, valleys or in dense stands of forest. If there is snow on the ground and you know where deer usually hole up under windy conditions, that will be a good place to look for tracks. Windy conditions make it difficult for deer to detect a hunter or tracker. Windy days can be productive. However, be very careful if you are hunting in an area with big trees. Falling trees and limbs can be deadly.

You may have heard or read stories about trackers running on a deer track or running deer down. After jumping a deer, there is generally little need to be cautious about noise until the tracks indicate that the deer has slowed down. A fast walk, a jog, or running will generally not further disturb the deer and may indeed put you closer to the deer when he does slow down.

BUT, BE CAREFUL! Safe gun handling must always be top priority. Falling down with a loaded gun can be hazardous to your health!

Caution should also be used to avoid exhaustion and excessive sweating even if you are in top physical shape. Hypothermia can be dangerous to anyone. If you are not in good physical condition, you certainly need to be careful in the woods and have a way to communicate with your hunting buddies.

Sometimes, it may be possible to take a deer that has grown accustom to the sounds of a slow pursuer by suddenly shifting to a fast, noisy style of travel. Sometimes this confuses a deer, and you may walk up on it. Use care in the rhythm of your steps. Listen to the sounds of other hunters that approach you in the woods. You will quickly notice that most hunters walk through the woods producing a rather steady, crunch, crunch rhythm of sound. Pay attention to the sounds of deer moving in the woods. The sounds of their walking have a different cadence and are more halting than are the sounds of a walking hunter. There may be definite advantages in trying to sound like a moving deer.

Deer are sprint runners. When jumped, research has found that bucks run an average of 60 yards before stopping to look back. Does stop running in even shorter distances. Deer generally spring short distances, stop, and then walk, although big bucks during the rut will sometimes take off seeming intent on heading out of the country. It is possible, however, that these bucks are outside of their normal home range on an excursion looking for does.

A deer that is jumped by a tracker rarely smells the tracker and often does not get a good look at the tracker. I have found that stopping and snorting like a deer may help keep a buck from running too far after being jumped. If a buck jumps up because he hears you, he may not know exactly where or what you are. Blowing, snorting or bleating like another deer is likely to diminish his alarm and perhaps make him curious. Deer blow when they are trying to catch the scent of a person or other animal that approaches. If a deer scents you, it usually won't blow; it will sneak away or run. Stay still for 10 or 15 minutes after jumping a deer and blowing. Use your eyes and binoculars to search for the buck. He may come back to check to see if you are another deer. Again, patience with slow and deliberate movements works best.

If you have the physical conditioning and stamina, it is possible given enough time to "dog" a deer and keep making him run until he tires. A buck is apt to run farther before stopping if jumped more than once. I prefer to go slow to avoid this. However, if a fast tracker pushes a buck until he tires, a buck may eventually slow down and stay just ahead of the tracker like a rabbit in front of a beagle. If this happens, chances of seeing the buck improve as he is sooner or later likely to step into an opening where he can seen and shot.

After a jumped buck slows back down to a walk, it is time to return to the task of concentrating on serious tracking. When tracks begin to meander around brush piles, downed trees, small knolls, or other objects, concentrate every effort on looking for the deer and making no noise. Meandering tracks are a sure sign that the deer is looking for a place to bed down. This is the time to catch him in his bed. Pay attention to the wind and high ground where a buck would be likely to bed.

**I tracked this buck for several hours and shot him when he got up from his bed.**

Once you have mastered the basic skills of tracking, you should find that you are coming up on deer that are either lying in their beds or standing looking at you. If you continue to see only running deer while tracking or just their tails, you are still moving too fast, making too much noise, or both.

If you really concentrate on your tracking and stay on a track for a full day, you will find that it takes a tremendous amount of mental and physical effort. You will be TIRED when you get back to camp! But, be assured, if you keep at it, you will see deer and develop skills that you be proud of. You might even take a really big buck.

**Arnold Lagrow with 240 lb. buck taken in Maine.**

# Every Day is Not a Day for Tracking

Unfortunately for the avid tracker, ideal tracking conditions frequently exist for only a few days each season even in northern states. One solution is to hole up in camp with a few buddies and a deck of cards. For me, hunting season just takes too long to come and passes too quickly to spend daylight hours in camp. Changing tactics to adjust to hunting conditions is the most productive solution and may even provide a refreshing change of pace.

On days when snow is either crusty or not deep enough to provide for quiet tracking, one solution is to team track. Team tracking in combination with standers on known runways can be quite effective, especially on noisy days. Team tracking involves use of a tracker following the track with one or two flankers on one or both sides of the tracker. Flankers must stay within sight of the tracker to prevent deer from passing between a flanker and the tracker and to make sure that everyone stays on the track when the track turns. The actual distance between the tracker and flankers must be constantly adjusted by the flankers as forest density changes. Flankers should spend all of their time looking for deer, keeping in sight and position with the tracker, and moving as quietly as possible. They should leave the tracking solely to the tracker in the center and remain slightly behind him, never in front of him.

Still hunting is at its best on those days when a steady, gentle rain is falling. Deer seem to be up moving around more than usual on these days. Although I have heard that scent carries well on wet, cool days and poorly on dry, hot days, I have walked within only a few feet of deer on rainy days. Either scent doesn't carry as well as has been reported in the rain, or wet ground simply permits a hunter to move so quietly that he has a significant advantage. The biggest disadvantage to hunting in the rain is that you are sure to get soaked unless you use special rain gear. Comfort can be maximized by careful choice and frequent changing of clothing.

Still hunting involves many of the same skills as tracking. The same quiet approach, attention to detail, caution about making quick movements, and total concentration are all required.

Hunting from stands, blinds, or other devices that provide a view and concealment can be very productive. Stands may overlook deer crossings or feeding areas. They may also be used in conjunction with natural or artificial rubs and scrapes, deer scents and lures, deer calls, or horn rattling. On those warm dry, or cold crisp sunny days of fall when the ground is free of snow and walking through the woods sounds like you are walking through a big bowl of corn flakes, tracking and still hunting are futile. If you want to be out there hunting, taking a stand is one of your best choices. To have a reasonable chance of success, your stand must be chosen wisely and you must have the patience to remain on your stand for long periods of time.

This is where experience having tracked deer in your hunting area will again pay off. Even if you don't catch up with a buck, every track you take should prove to be a valuable learning experience providing insight into travel routes, crossings, and activities of deer within your hunting area. Using this information when selecting stand sites should give you a definite edge and greater confidence which will help provide the patience necessary to wait and stay alert through the long hours of the day.

Hunting over bait has become very popular in some parts of the country and in hunting videos. Baiting is not for me. I refuse to participate. It changes the natural travel and behavioral patterns of deer. It causes abnormal and unhealthy concentrations of deer. Of course, it is popular because it works without a lot of effort on the part of the hunter. It is not particularly conducive to development of hunting skills.

In some parts of the country, groups of hunters will get together and conduct "deer drives." These range from very loosely organized operations involving as few as two or three hunters to major strategic exercises involving scores of hunters, vehicles, noise makers, and two way radios. Again, knowing the travel patterns and behavior of deer in the area is invaluable information for making successful deer drives.

I have taken part in deer drives from the simple to the complex. Through time and experience, I have come to shy away from these. In many cases, the odds of some hunter in the group getting a deer are increased by cooperation. However, it has always seemed to me that the individual odds of any particular hunter getting a deer are also changed such that the novice hunter has a better chance than normal while more experienced hunters diminish their chances. Even "deer drives" require sound planning to be consistently successful. In some cases, more than half of all hunting hours may be spent standing around planning and regrouping. In the worst cases, concentration of hunters in small areas can result in a dangerous situation when several hunters shoot at the same deer from different directions.

Large concentrations of hunters draw a lot of attention. Even when hunters are well behaved, large hunter groups conducting deer drives in populated areas generally do little to promote good relationships with the public and result in more posted land. When there happens to be even one "bad apple" in the group, the whole group and hunters in general are commonly blamed by the general public for any bad behavior observed.

I have also hunted deer with dogs in the southern U.S. It seemed a lot like rabbit hunting, only on a grander scale. Once again, it is important to know the travel routes that deer will take in order to optimally position standers on dog hunts.

All, in all, I get the greatest enjoyment out of getting into the woods and hunting alone or with a few good friends. I feel that this helps one focus on developing the skills that, for me at least, brings the greatest personal satisfaction. Everyone gets something a little different out of their hunting experiences, the main thing is for you to get as much enjoyment out of your time in the field as you can. People do have to work within their own physical limitations.

So, try to get the most satisfaction possible from your hunting experiences regardless of the style of hunting that you choose. There will never be enough deer seasons in a lifetime.

# Not Getting Lost and Not Worrying About It

A hunter who is serious about tracking down a buck can't be spending time worrying about getting lost. He must concentrate 80 to 90 percent of his effort on the task of looking for deer and being quiet. The GPS equipment now available can make navigation across the landscape an easy chore. However, you do have to learn to use the equipment and be able to use it day or night under field conditions. If you can't use it, the best equipment in the world won't take you home.

A hunter can follow deer tracks day after day without ever getting a glimpse of a deer if he is so scared of getting lost that his eyes remain glued to his compass or he spends all of his time looking at landmarks. On the other hand, getting lost can cost you a great deal of lost time and anxiety. In the most remote areas or when extreme panic sets in, getting lost can even result in a life threatening situation.

If you ever get lost, DO NOT PANIC! Sit down, calm down, and think rationally about your problem. Don't use your feet. Use your head! The greatest danger when a person feels lost is generally the danger of exposure and hypothermia which increases when panic sets in and sweating occurs. Remember, the greatest distance and time back to your camp or vehicle is no farther or longer than the distance and time that you have traveled since you started the day. Unless, you walked in a straight line away from your vehicle, the distance is actually shorter. Don't make it farther by heading off wildly in the wrong direction. Keep in mind that nearly all lost hunters are found within 72 hours. Even without food and water, a hunter who keeps his wits should be prepared and able to survive for 72 hours in whitetail country.

Every hunter should carry a space blanket in his pack or jacket at all times. Space blankets are readily available at sport shops. They are inexpensive, light weight, and an effective way to keep warm in emergency situations.

Few areas exist within the continental United States where travel in a straight line will not soon bring you to a road, railroad, power line, or some other link to civilization. Logging roads head for public highways. Small streams flow into larger streams. Larger streams always eventually lead into valley bottoms where agriculture, people, and roads will usually be found.

However, in some areas, stream bottoms can be difficult or impossible to negotiate. Studying maps and getting in the field for pre-season scouting is the best way to ensure that you are aware of dangerous or problem areas before you ever set out to hunt.

Swamps are perhaps the most difficult terrain in which to keep from getting turned around. Thick cover and flatness of the terrain can make it very difficult to view landmarks while blow downs, water and mud may make passage in some directions difficult or impossible.

When landmarks are few or when a hunter doesn't pay attention to the direction he is travelling, he will usually tend to turn in one direction more often than the other as he is forced to move around obstacles in his path. This tendency results in the common phenomenon of walking in a circle.

A hunter can maintain a straight course of travel in several ways. He can frequently refer to his GPS or compass. He can orient to the sun or other celestial bodies, a mountain peak, or some other prominent landmark. Or, when landmarks and a clear sky are not visible, a hunter can always use a line of sight means of keeping a straight course. To use this method, locate trees or other objects in your path ahead and line these up with objects that you have just passed. Move ahead to the furthest object located and repeat the process until you get out of the woods. Few areas exist where steady progress in a single direction will not bring you out of the woods within a short time. Even with today's high-tech GPS units, it is wise to always carry a compass and become expert at traditional methods of orienteering. You can never tell when technology might fail you.

You will read accounts about telling direction by observing which side of the trees moss is growing on and the direction in which fallen trees are lying. Personally, I don't intend to stake my life on those methods.

If you don't know where you are when you go into the woods, you are lost before you get started. Getting lost can almost always be avoided by taking time to learn your hunting area. Learn relative positions of mountains, streams, roads, swamps, and other landforms. The best way to orient yourself before entering a new hunting area or even to gain a better understanding of the lay of the land in your old stomping grounds is to look at a map. Google Earth and other on-line and electronic mapping programs are fantastic tools that will quickly help you get a mental picture of the landscape in your head if not in your pocket. When possible, drive completely around the area you plan to hunt so that you can recognize landmarks when you see them and can better interpret the markings on your topographic maps. Take GPS readings and set way points or landmarks at locations along the road where you might come out if you were tracking a deer. Record these as way points in your GPS. These will prove particularly useful if you need to come out of the woods by the shortest route.

It is essential to learn to use a compass, GPS and a topographic map if you intend to become a serious hunter and tracker. It is not hard. You don't need a college degree in surveying to learn enough about maps and compasses to get out of the woods when and where you want to.

Don't get too cocky! Even if you become an expert in orienteering, accidents can happen. Be sure to let someone, preferably your hunting buddies, know roughly where you plan to hunt and when you plan to return before setting out. Even if you happen to change your plans during the course of the day, your hunting buddies should have enough information to reasonably define a search area if you don't return in a timely manner. By the same token, if you should return from the woods early and your buddies are not around, don't just head for home without leaving a message. It is aggravating (to put it mildly) to spend valuable time worrying and searching for someone only to find later that he was safe and sound at home in bed with his wife.

Topographic maps and compasses are readily available through local sporting goods dealers and are inexpensive. In the age of GPS and digital satellite imagery, compasses still provide a reliable back up system for navigation. Don't buy the cheapest compass that you can find. I prefer a good quality, liquid filled compass whose arrow doesn't dance to all points of the compass when I get it out of my pocket. Some hunter's prefer a little compass that they pin to their jackets, but these have a tendency to get pulled off and lost. Don't forget to keep your compass away from your gun barrel and other metallic objects or it won't work properly. It is also wise to determine the current magnetic North declination and adjust your compass if it is adjustable so that they work properly with topo maps.

88

**Maine deer camp.: A lot of good times.**

# Tracking Wounded Deer

Sooner or later every hunter will have to search for a wounded deer. A few precautions and techniques will maximize your likelihood of finding it.

After taking a shot at a buck, particularly if it is any distance away, pause for a moment. Carefully note landmarks near the spot where the deer was at the time of the shot, as well as landmarks at the spot from which you shot. Tying a piece of surveying tape to a branch takes only a second and can be invaluable if you have to return to take another look at the direction that you were shooting in. Enter a way point into your GPS unit.

It should go without saying, never shoot at a deer and leave the field or woods without checking to see if you hit the deer. Even if a deer doesn't seem to react to your shot, always check. It is not unusual for deer shot cleanly through the heart to jump and run 50 to 100 yards before dropping. Deer shot through the lungs may run even further. Over the years, I have known more than one deer that has been left to rot because someone was too lazy to walk a few yards to check and see if they hit the deer.

Once you locate the spot where you think the deer was when you took the shot, begin looking for blood, hair, and tracks. There have been times when I have had to get down on my hands and knees to see and track tiny blood droplets The color of vegetation can make spotting blood difficult. I also find it very difficult to look for tracks and other signs of disturbance while at the same time looking for blood. At least for me, it works better if I can have one of my hunting buddies concentrate on looking for blood behind me as I track. This helps confirm that I am staying on the right track when tracking under difficult bare ground conditions.

Pay attention to the spatter pattern and shape of blood drops on the ground and vegetation. You can learn to use these to tell the direction in which a wounded deer has traveled. Blood streaks and secondary splatter have linear elements that indicate the direction of blood impact which parallels the direction that the wounded deer traveled.

**Blood spatter reveals the direction of travel.**

If you have to track in a bog having pitcher plants and sun dews, you may find that the red colors of the plants closely match the color of blood. Red maple leaves also can make seeing blood difficult.

If you are color blind, you may have a serious problem seeing blood. Commercial products containing luminol can help on tricky blood trails where only small droplets of blood have been deposited. The blue luminescence given off when luminol contacts blood requires fairly dim or dark light conditions to be seen. Color blind people are generally able to see blue. So, products containing luminol can be a big help to them.

There are limitations to these products. They are hard to use in bright light. The luminescence only lasts about 30 seconds. You have to mix the luminol products in the field because once mixed luminol has to be used within 6-8 hours. But, it works and is a good thing to have in your hunting kit.

Patience is absolutely necessary on a difficult blood trail. If you look for blood and don't find any, flag the spot where you thought the deer was and enter another way point into your GPS. After the spot is flagged, begin to carefully search the ground and vegetation while traveling in an every widening circle around the flagged spot until you pick up sign. You can also use your GPS unit to make sure that there are no "holes" in your search pattern. Turn on the "Tracking" feature on your GPS so that you can track your movements. Use the GPS unit to ensure that you make a systematic search of the area.

Never give up before you have made every reasonable effort to find sign.

Blood and hair have different appearances depending upon the location of a wound. Blood from a lung wound will be bright red and frothy while blood from a stomach wound will produce dark colored blood and maybe stomach contents. Look for bone chips. White hair indicates a wound along the belly while dark hairs indicate a wound near the top of the back. If you have learned to call your shots you should already have a pretty good idea of where the shot should have struck the deer.

Heavily bleeding deer will usually head down hill and towards water. Loss of blood makes animals thirsty. It is not uncommon to find a wounded deer or dead deer laying in or near a stream, pond or other water body. If you find that you are unable to follow a blood trail, always make a thorough search of nearby streambeds or lake shores before giving up the search. Again, making a systematic search in ever increasing circles or in a grid pattern is the best way to insure a thorough search of an area.

It is not always wise to hastily follow wounded deer. If a good blood trail is present and weather conditions are not working to erase the trail, it is usually wise to wait 15-20 minutes before beginning to track the deer. This gives the deer time to calm down and become less alert to your approach. Wounded deer typically don't run very far before lying down unless they are chased. Often they will simply lay down and die. When they are pursued, adrenaline may keep them going for a long distance even when critically wounded.

Some hunters recommend waiting 4 or 5 hours or more before tracking a wounded deer. Just remember, older trails are harder to follow and even under cool weather conditions deer will begin to bloat and spoil in as little as 4 or 5 hours.

# Equipment & Clothing

It is important to minimize noise when tracking. Wool, cotton, flannel, and felt clothing is quietest. Branches and briars scraping against wool make little noise compared to most other materials. If you can make a scraping sound by scratching your finger nails against an article of clothing, it is too noisy to wear while tracking.

It is also preferable to wear boots with soft rubber soles. Soft, flexible soles let the hunter feel sticks and other objects underfoot before putting enough weight on them to make them crack. If you wear anything on your shooting hand, it must not slow down or in any way hamper your ability to shoot.

Other than meeting these functional requirements, choice of clothing only matters in as far as it keeps you comfortable by keeping you dry, warm, or cool as the case may be. When setting off for an all day hunt in cool or cold weather, I always carry a small wool day pack in which I carry a set of clean long underwear in a plastic garbage bag. The plastic bag doubles as a container for the heart and liver when I get a deer. I have found that taking off my clothes on a mountain side even in the snow and cold and replacing wet underwear with dry provides instant comfort. It is amazing how rapidly warmth returns even when outer garments remain damp. A hunter must be comfortable in order to hunt effectively.

I also carry a lunch, some nylon rope, a little surveying tape for marking locations, and a plastic container of drinking water or soda in my day pack. In my jacket, I carry a good compass, a GPS unit, a small pair of field glasses, a cigarette lighter, and toilet paper. I prefer to carry my shells in a belt case having a foam insert that keeps them from clinking together while walking. I also carry a sharp four inch hunting knife in a belt sheath. A four inch knife is the longest knife that you usually need to carry. Longer knives are too big and awkward for effective use inside of the body cavity of a deer. They at best make field dressing more difficult and at worst can result in cut hands or fingers.

This equipment works well for me. However, most hunters will have their own preferences. The main point is: be prepared. It will be more comfortable if you try to manage this without requiring a pack horse to haul your gear around.

Don't forget your TRACKOMETER. It provides a valuable scouting tool for studying the tracks of white-tailed deer. If you don't have one, you can order one at WWW.TRACKOMETER.COM.

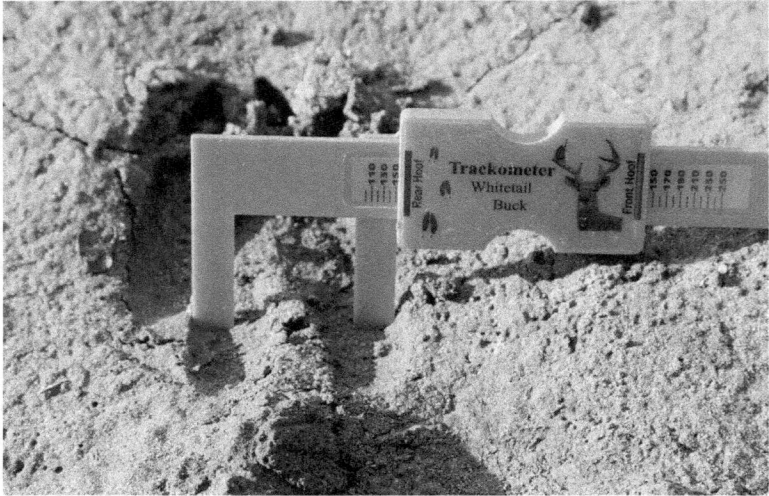

**Tracks may provide the key to understanding deer movements in your favorite hunting area. The more that you learn about white-tails, the more you will enjoy scouting and hunting for them.**

**The trail doesn't end here. There will always be more to learn. Get out in the field. Have fun and good luck!**

**Most of us will always need the touch of a little luck. But, the hunting and outdoor skills we gain through training and experience will bring the most consistent hunting success and a self satisfaction that will last for a lifetime.**

www.ingramcontent.com/pod-product-compliance
Lightning Source LLC
LaVergne TN
LVHW051700080426
835511LV00017B/2656